PUBLICATIONS OF THE UNIVERSITY
OF MANCHESTER

CLASSICAL SERIES No. VI

POLITICAL INTERPRETATIONS IN GREEK LITERATURE

Published by the University of Manchester at the University Press
[H. M. McKechnie, M.A., Secretary], 8–10 Wright Street, Manchester 15

POLITICAL INTERPRETATIONS IN GREEK LITERATURE

BY

T. B. L. WEBSTER

Hulme Professor of Greek in the University of Manchester

MANCHESTER UNIVERSITY PRESS

1948

To
A. M. W.

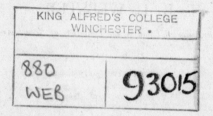
THIS BOOK IS PRODUCED IN COMPLETE
CONFORMITY WITH THE AUTHORISED
ECONOMY STANDARDS

PREFACE

THIS book grew in my mind during the later years of the war and the first draft was written in the summer of 1945. My object was to try and see what were the essential ideas of ancient democracy, how they arose, what were the difficulties encountered by full democracy and what the remedies proposed. The kind reception accorded to my *Greek Interpretations* suggested that the same method might be used here, i.e. long quotations from Greek literature with commentary. I am not a historian or a philosopher and my object is not to write a history of Greek political thought, but to show how the essential ideas of democracy at various stages of development were expressed by Greek poets and prose-writers from Homer to Aristotle, sketching in the history as far as it is necessary to explain my texts. I have attempted, as far as possible, to standardise translations of essential words, usually giving the Greek word in transliterated form. I should like finally to express my thanks to my wife for much help at all stages, to Dr. E. J. F. James for reading my manuscript and for making many suggestions which I have gratefully adopted, and to Mr. H. M. McKechnie for his skill in overcoming speedily the difficulties of present-day book production.

T. B. L. WEBSTER.

MANCHESTER,

1947.

CONTENTS

HOMER

GREEK literature begins for us with the *Iliad* and the *Odyssey*, in which signs of future political development can already be observed. There is no space here to argue in full the case for dating the *Iliad* and *Odyssey* in the ninth/eighth century B.C., produced possibly by a single poet for a great national festival of the Greeks who had migrated to Asia Minor during and after the disturbances usually called the Dorian invasion. The commercial expansion of these Ionian cities had not yet begun and therefore these Greeks loved to hear of their glorious past, particularly the stories of Troy, one of the great sea-raiding exploits of the Viking Mycenaean empire, in the early twelfth century B.C. Homer's material for the *Iliad* and the *Odyssey* consisted partly of minstrels' lays, which went back not only to the preceding Mycenaean civilisation, but beyond to the Minoan civilisation of Crete; in part, like all writers of history (and the ancient Greek was always less shy of history in modern dress than we are), he filled in his story with the social customs of his own time; this means that we have to distinguish in Homer between two forms of political organisation: the military organisation of Agamemnon's Mycenaean empire and the civil organisation of the Greek cities of Ionia in the ninth to eighth century B.C.

Agamemnon's empire consisted of " many islands and all Argos " and the sceptre which he carried had been handed down to him from his grandfather, who received it from Zeus, the king of the gods. " The kingship is his by hereditary right, he is the leader in war, and at his side are the council of elders and the

army assembly." [1]   The army assembly is the oldest
form of popular assembly ; the king summoned it in
order to deliberate on important matters ; the assembly
gave voice to its opinion by cries, but the decision
rested with the king alone.   The commanders of the
local contingents (Odysseus, Achilles, etc.), who were
themselves called " kings ", formed the council of
elders when the king wanted advice.   Each of these
vassals had his own " companions ", his friends who
messed with him but who also acted as his " servants ".
When he conquered a country, the king took the
largest part, after him the noblemen took specially
selected parts and the people divided the rest.   With
the break-up of the Mycenaean empire after the Dorian
invasion, the vassals of the king of Mycenae became
independent kings of their own territory and their
" companions " gradually became more and more independent, which finally led to aristocratic government
instead of kingship.   But Agamemnon's Aegean empire
survived as a memory, perpetuated by Homer, to
inspire later Greeks with dreams of Aegean unity.

Professor Rostovtzeff draws the following general
picture of Greece in Homeric times : [2]

The political organisation of Greece was dictated by
the geographical and economic conditions.   Nature had
divided her into small economic units, and she was incapable of creating large political systems.   So it had been
during the prevalence of the Aegean culture, and so it still
remained.   Each valley was self-centred, and its inhabitants jealously guarded their pasture and arable land.   The
best parts of the country, especially its rich valleys, are
open to the sea and shut in by land—separated from the
central high valleys and plateaux by formidable barriers.

[1] Nilsson, *Homer and Mycenae*, 221 f.
[2] *Orient and Greece*, 181 f., 184 f.

They are more in touch with those neighbours from whom the sea divides them than with those whom the land brings near them. It is easier for them to exchange goods and ideas by sea than by land. Hence civilisation develops quickly on the coast but slowly in the centre of the country. The type of life is however the same in all parts. Stocks, and portions of stocks, form petty political units which keep jealous guard of their independence. To protect themselves and their property against attack they build fortified refuges on the hill-tops and these by degrees are converted into cities [*poleis*], which offer markets for their produce, a centre of religious life, and a residence for their kings, leaders in war, and priests. The city becomes a focus of a larger or smaller territory, inhabited by farmers and shepherds who live either in detached houses and cottages scattered over the country, or together in villages [*demes*]. . . . The farming of the Homeric Greeks consists mainly of agriculture and stock-raising, but horticulture, especially the growing of vines and olive-trees, is also developed by degrees. The last industry, however, is only in its early stages ; Greece is still a land of cornfields and flocks. Cattle, swine, sheep and goats are common animals ; to own horses is a privilege of rich and noble families. The stock owned by such families is sometimes very numerous, and a man's wealth is measured by his head of cattle. Little buying is done, and that unwillingly ; most necessaries are produced at home. Domestic manufacture supplies not only food but clothes, furniture, agricultural implements and foot-gear. The whole family works ; the men plough, sow, plant trees, reap, mow, look after the cattle, milk the cows and goats, make butter and cheese, go out hunting ; the women spin, weave, embroider, wash linen and clothes, cook the food. Hard work is no humiliation and is not considered burdensome or oppressive. Odysseus boasts that he had no superior in reaping and mowing, that he could build a ship and his own bed and adorn it with cunning patterns. . . . The slaves and houseless hired servants form a part of the household as a social and productive unit. Though the hardest and most repulsive labour falls to their lot, yet they are neither machines nor animals. Like the other members of the family they come under the patronage and protection of the household gods, and humane treatment is secured to them by religion and custom. Only the more difficult work is done by professional craftsmen who are paid for their labour.

The *Odyssey* presents two notable accounts of early Greek city life. The Phaeacians, who finally conveyed Odysseus home to Ithaca after his wanderings,

formerly dwelt in the wide dancing-places of Hypereia near the Cyclops, the proud men, who did them damage and were more powerful. Godlike Nausithous led them away from there and settled them in Scheria, far from bread-eating men, and drove a wall round the city, and built houses, and made temples of the gods, and divided up the land. But he had already gone to Hades, and Alcinous was then king, who knew wisdom from the gods (vi. 4 f.).

The Phaeacian city of Scheria is therefore pictured as a wanderers' settlement at the times of the migrations after the Dorian invasion or perhaps even later.

There is a fair harbour on either side of the city with a narrow entrance. The curved ships are drawn up along the road ; for each man has his station, and there is their assembly place about the fair temple of Poseidon and it is built of quarried stone (vi. 263 f.).

In the morning, after Odysseus' arrival, Alcinous " led him to the assembly place of the Phaeacians which they had made by the ships, and they came and sat upon the polished stones " (vii. 4 f.), and the " leaders and counsellors of the Phaeacians " were then summoned by herald.

On the procedure of such a council, the second book

of the *Odyssey* is enlightening. There, Telemachus, Odysseus' son, sends heralds to summon the nobles of Ithaca to the assembly. He then goes and sits on his father's throne (i.e. the king has a special seat) and the *gerontes* (" old ones ", used of the nobles although some of them are quite young) give place to him. The oldest member of the Council speaks first (perhaps that is his privilege) : " Hear me now, Ithacans, what I say. We have had no assembly or session since goodly Odysseus went in the hollow ships. Now who has summoned us ? " This shows that any noble has the right to summon the Council and it appears from the end of the scene that any noble has the right to dismiss it. The full course of the debate can now be read in Mr. Rieu's admirable translation. Telemachus, the king's son, asks for a ship to take him to Pylos and Sparta to get news of his father, and his request is refused. It is quite clear that the king's son has no special rights on this Council except the right to sit in his father's chair ; the government is, in practice, in the hands of the nobles and the Council of aristocrats has already developed its rules of procedure.

In the days of the Trojan War, the justification for the king's pre-eminence was his prowess in war ; thus in the *Iliad*, the Lycian chief Sarpedon asks (xii. 310) :

Glaucus, why are we honoured most in Lycia—given front seats, the best meat, and full cups—all look on us as gods—and we pasture a great reservation by the banks of Xanthus, orchard-land and ploughland ? Therefore now we must stand in the forefront of the Lycians and meet the flaming battle, that one of the mailed Lycians may say : " Our kings of Lycia are not inglorious. They eat the fat sheep and drink the honeyed wine. But they have a noble strength, when they fight in the forefront of the Lycians."

When such special needs for a single strong command as war or migration no longer remained, the king's essential function was gone and the vassals became proportionately more powerful.

It is probably right to assume that in the account of the army assembly in the second book of the *Iliad* (ii. 200) the colouring and character-drawing reflects Homer's own world. It contains the earliest portrait of a popular opponent of the established government : Thersites (his father's name is not given, therefore he is a man of the people) was the ugliest man who came to Troy, lame in one leg and his shoulders bent over his chest ; " he knew many words in his heart, but they were all disorderly, for he strove with the kings ". On this occasion he shouted aloud :

Son of Atreus, of what do you complain or what do you lack ? Your quarters are full of bronze and there are many chosen women in your quarters whom we Achaeans give to you first, whenever we capture a citadel. . . . Let us go home and leave him [Agamemnon] here in Troy to digest his spoils, that he may see whether we too help anything or not.

Thereupon Odysseus told him to be silent and beat him with a staff on the back and shoulders, and the crowd said : " Verily Odysseus has done ten thousand good things . . . but now this is the best thing of all that he has done among the Argives in that he stopped this wordy insulter from speaking in the assembly." The picture is clear enough : the brave man who spoke the unpopular truth deserted by the place-seeking multitude and caricatured by the aristocratic poet. Nevertheless, criticism of the aristocratic government by a man of the people had already begun and Homer recorded it ; the individual had raised his voice against the state with a sturdy independence.

Thus at the beginning of Greek literature in the ninth century B.C. in a small feudal world of kings, princes, and retainers, we can already see the germ of later development. First, the king of kings disappears when he can no longer justify himself as a war-lord ; then the individual kings in their turn, unable to justify special privileges by special services, sink to the level of their " companions ", and the forms of government by an aristocratic council are moulded. Thersites, cruelly caricatured and ruthlessly manhandled, is the beginning of a democratic opposition to aristocratic misuse of power.

II

HESIOD AND SOLON

THE second Greek poet whose works have survived is Hesiod, who lived at Ascra in Boeotia in the late eighth century B.C. It may have been very little later than Homer but he seems to us to belong to a different world because his *Works and Days* is set in contemporary Ascra, whereas the *Iliad* and *Odyssey*, however much may be gleaned from them about contemporary Ionia, are set in the heroic past and contain material drawn directly from the heroic past. Hesiod writes in a small town in Boeotia organised in the typical Greek way as an independent *polis*, a little city-state governed by a landowning aristocracy, in which seafaring trade is beginning to become important.

Various changes distinguish eighth-century Ascra from the world depicted by Homer. In the first place Hesiod speaks of " kings " in the plural instead of the " king ", implying that monarchy has already yielded to aristocracy ; secondly, the small farmer and the seafaring trader play a part in this society and are as interesting to the poet as the hereditary large-scale landowners ; thirdly, poetry no longer looks backward to the great deeds of the past, but finds in present-day life a sufficiently exciting subject to satisfy the demands of the understanding audience. The Homeric singer always acted his part, and the long speeches of advice (e.g. Phoenix to Achilles in the ninth book of the *Iliad*) were recited in character ; Hesiod, brought up in this tradition, took the bold step of being himself instead of impersonating some bygone hero, and sang of his own lawsuit with his brother. This no doubt resounded loud enough in the little town of Ascra, but Hesiod gave it a far wider significance by making it part of a more general consideration of the position held by the small farmer, the merchant, and the hereditary land-owning nobility.

Our knowledge of Hesiod and his family is largely derived from an autobiographical passage in his *Works and Days* (630 f.) :

Wait for the coming of spring to put to sea and then drag your swift ship to the sea and put a fitting load in it that you may bring profit home, as my father and yours, you great fool Perses, used to sail in ships, lacking enriching livelihood, who once came even here, having voyaged far over the sea, leaving Cyme of Aeolis, in his black ship, not fleeing from riches or wealth or prosperity but from crippling poverty which Zeus gives to men, and he settled near Helicon in a miserable village, Ascra, crippling in winter, bitter in summer, and never enriching. But do you, Perses, remember that all work should be done in its due season, particularly seafaring. Refuse a small ship, have your cargo put in a big ship. The cargo is bigger and there is greater gain upon gain, if the winds keep off their crippling blasts. Since you are turning your greedy mind to commerce and want to escape debts and cruel hunger, I will show you the measures of the resounding sea though I am not wise about seafaring or ships, for I never yet sailed in a ship over the broad sea except from Euboea to Aulis where once the Achaeans, biding a storm, mustered many people from holy Greece against Troy the land of fair women. There I crossed to Chalcis to the funeral games of warlike Amphidamas ; the sons of that great man had advertised many contests. There I say I was victorious with a hymn and won an eared tripod. That I dedicated to the Muses of Helicon, where they first put me on the path of sweet song.

From this we learn that Hesiod's father belonged to a family which had left Greece in the migrations for

B

Cyme in Asia Minor and had apparently not made good in the east ; Hesiod's father was unsuccessful as a merchant (this is the meaning of " used to sail in ships ") and returned to Greece, where he was given a settlement at Ascra. Hesiod tells us elsewhere (*Theog.* 22) : " [The Muses] taught Hesiod a fair song as he pastured his sheep beneath lovely Helicon." We can therefore assume that Hesiod's father became a farmer and Hesiod in due course a shepherd, but that he forsook this life for poetry, performing in international contests such as that in Euboea which he describes and which can be dated on independent testimony to the late eighth century. A further piece of autobiography brings us right into the town-life of Ascra (*Works and Days*, 27 f.) :

Perses, put this in your heart and do not let strife that rejoices in evil keep your soul from work, watching for quarrels, listening to gossip. There is no season for quarrels and gossip when a man has not substance in corn, which the earth brings season after season. If you have plenty, you can stir quarrels and strife to gain others' goods. But let us forthwith decide the quarrel by straight decisions [*dike*] which come from Zeus and are the best. For long ago we divided our inheritance and you won much other plunder by flattering the bribe-greedy kings, who propose to judge this suit.

When Hesiod's father died, the division of the inheritance, the plot of land which he had been given, including both arable land and pasture land for Hesiod's sheep, gave rise to a lawsuit between the brothers, Hesiod and Perses, which Perses won by bribing the " bribe-greedy kings " to give crooked judgment.

The poem is a direct sermon, in form, to his brother, in fact to all the free elements in Hesiod's world, nobles, traders, small farmers. The gospel which he preaches is threefold : the city must be founded on justice, prosperity only comes from hard work, and hard work must be guided by knowledge ; all three are given a divine sanction ; Justice is the daughter of Zeus, Zeus made hard work necessary by hiding riches from men, and the Muses, who are the daughters of Zeus, know " the measures of things ". A couple of lines from the *Theogony* (902) show how closely the three conceptions are linked in Hesiod's mind : " [Zeus] married lovely Themis, who gave birth to the Seasons, Good Order [*Eunomia*], Justice [*Dike*] and blooming Peace, who mark the seasons for men's labours." Hesiod casts his picture of the life of the city into the form of a family tree. The wife of Zeus is Themis. Themis means " ordaining " or " something ordained ". When the king of the gods marries the personified principle of " ordaining ", their offspring is three further personifications, which have a significance both in nature and in human affairs. In nature they are the Seasons ; in human affairs they are Good Order (*Eunomia*), Justice (*Dike*), and Peace. The meaning of Peace is clear ; Good Order in Hesiod means, I think, the possession of Good Customs (*nomoi*)[1]—the later development of the meaning of *nomos* will be dealt with below. *Dike* perhaps originally meant the " cast " of the judge's sceptre as he delivered a judgment ; on many Greek occasions holding a sceptre, rod, or wand gave one the right to speak and the rod was thrown down when the speech was over. From this the meaning of *dike* developed in two directions, first to signify things connected with the act of judging such as " judgment, plea, satisfaction, penalty, or lawsuit " and secondly to mean " justice " in the abstract. This second use occurs already in Homer : " the blessed

[1] See now Ehrenberg, *Aspects of the Ancient World*, 70 f.

gods do not love cruel deeds but honour justice and the fair dealing of men " (*Odyssey*, XIV, 83). Hesiod personifies justice and makes her a season ; by this he means both that the forces of order are the same in the natural as in the human world and that Justice being a Season can reward the just with good weather for their crops and punish the unjust with storms and unseasonable weather.

Hesiod sees the social and political system (Good Order and Justice), peace and prosperity (both are included in Peace), and successful agriculture (produced by hard labour and knowledge of the Seasons) as part of the same divine dispensation. The Seasons are the daughters of Zeus and their names are Justice, Good Order, and Peace ; social and economic orderliness is grounded in the orderliness of the Universe. The wise man, who directs his agriculture and seafaring to suit the Seasons, directs his political and social life by Justice, which distinguishes man from the beasts (*Works and Days*, 274) :

Perses, put this in your heart and listen to Justice and forget violence altogether. For Zeus appointed this custom [*nomos*] for men : that fish and beasts and winged birds should eat each other because there is no Justice among them, but to men he gave Justice which is for the best.

A few lines before (260) Hesiod has said that the people (*demos*) pay for the madness of their kings, who turn aside in their folly and give crooked judgments (*dike*). Justice then is the concern of the whole body politic, because the whole body politic pays with war and famine (220 ff.) for the crooked judgments of their nobles. Thus, for Hesiod's time we can reasonably speak of a whole body politic comprising small farmers and merchants as well as the hereditary aristocracy, a *polis* held together by *dike*, in which poetry is not merely an ornament of the king's court but may also be the mouthpiece of the oppressed.

In the Greek cities of Asia Minor, the development was probably quicker than in Ascra in backward Boeotia, partly because of the richness of the soil, partly because of the proximity of highly cultured Oriental kingdoms, such as the Hittites, the Phrygians, and the Lydians, and later the Persians. The desire to trade both inwards with the Oriental kingdoms and outwards over the sea produced three changes with far-reaching consequences, all of which took place slightly later in the cities of Greece itself. First, wine and oil proved good for export and landowners turned over from corn and pasture to vineyards and olive-yards. Secondly, wine and oil must be exported in containers, and the Greek pottery industry developed, first as a natural ancillary, then as an industry on its own, producing fine cups and jars for export. Thirdly, the growth of trade made an easy medium of exchange necessary ; in the small self-supporting community the farmer pays the itinerant craftsman in kind and when he takes his corn or animal to the town he brings back the results of barter. But the olive-grower of Smyrna does not wait for payment until his olive-oil has been bartered in Trebizond ; the merchant must give him a *quid pro quo* in Smyrna, a lump of precious metal which he can barter for something he needs ; when this lump of metal bears a state seal to guarantee its value, it is a coin. All these changes increased the class distinctions in the city. The olive and vineyard owners and the potters ran their concerns on slave labour ; they, the shipowners, and the merchants became a power which threatened the agricultural aristocracy ; the smallholders, unable to adopt modern methods, found it more and more difficult to live and often paid their debts with their persons.

The echoes of these struggles can be heard in the surviving fragments of the lyric poets ; the songs of Archilochus of Paros, who was perhaps a contemporary of Hesiod, and of Alcaeus of Lesbos, who lived at the end of the seventh century, were sung after dinner by their friends and became the expression of a group rather than of an individual. Archilochus was an adventurer and cared nothing for the traditional honour of the aristocratic families of Paros, who boasted their descent from heroic ancestors :

> Not mine a general who is tall and swaggers,
>   with flowing locks and shaven chin.
> Give me a small one whose legs are staggered,
>   if he's firm on his feet and full of vim.
>
> (fr. 60)

> A perfect shield bedecks some Thracian now ;
> I had no choice ; I left it in a wood.
> Ah well, I saved my skin, so let it go !
>   A new one's just as good.
>
> (fr. 6, tr. Sir William Marris)

Here again we hear the voice of an opposition which demands something more solid than pedigree and the codes of aristocratic behaviour.

Alcaeus was an aristocratic landowner and went into exile after an unsuccessful battle against the merchant-prince Myrsilus, who became tyrant of Lesbos. This is a specimen of his political allegorical poetry :

> I don't understand the war of the winds ;
> one wave from this side rolling upon us,
> one wave from that, and we between
> are borne along in our black ship

Toiling against the towering storm.
The water washes the base of the mast,
the sail is holed by wind and rain,
and great are the rents upon it.

A new wave rises higher than all,
rises, bringing us toil upon toil.
Strengthen the bulwarks with all speed
and run for a sheltered shore.

May not the softness of fear befall us.
The mighty struggle is clear to the eye.
Remember when we toiled before ;
now is the time for courage.

And may no cowardice bring us to shame before
our valiant fathers who lie underground. . . .

(fr. 1, 30, 120)

The development of Athens in the seventh century
was not essentially different from the development
that we have described, but our sources of information
are better and we can fill in rather more details. The
merchant class had won considerable victories over the
aristocracy before the end of this century. Probably
the most far-reaching was to secure the publication of
the laws of murder ; justice was thus no longer a secret
imparted to the aristocracy by the gods and administered by them as the sole possessors of this revelation,
but its principles were known by all who could read.
At the same time the magistracies and the right of
voting for magistracies, which had become annual, were
based not on heredity but on a property qualification.
Citizens who had enough money to serve in the cavalry
were eligible for magistracies ; citizens who had enough
money to serve in the heavy infantry formed the

electorate and the *ekklesia* or popular assembly, by which laws were passed. But the most influential body for political, religious, and judicial business was the Council of the Areopagus, which had grown out of the old Council of Elders and now contained ex-magistrates as well as representatives of the oldest families.

The property qualification was however based on land and, in order to enter the governing classes, the rich merchants had to buy land. They bought largely from the smallholders who were too poor to keep pace with modern improvements ; sometimes they sold their land, sometimes they borrowed money at extortionate rates and when they could not pay, lost both their land and their freedom. Some became tenants of the rich and paid five-sixths of their produce in rent. Whether enslaved, dispossessed, or rent-ridden tenants, they were unhappy and ready for a new deal. Aristotle thus describes the situation (*Athp.* 5) : " the many were enslaved to the few and the people resisted the nobles. Civil strife became violent and for a long time they beleaguered each other, until they both chose Solon as arbitrator and archon." This is the first instance of something like a popular revolution.

Solon's reforms were both economic and political.

Allotments of land which had been mortgaged to the rich were restored to the owners, and the debts were cancelled. . . . It was made illegal to advance money on the security of land or the landowner's person. . . . Export of corn was forbidden . . . to make speculative cultivation of arable land unprofitable and to simplify the transference of such land to smallholders . . . the capitalists' wealth was turned into a more profitable channel ; the growth of olive-trees for the export of oil was stimulated, and trade and industry in general were encouraged.[1]

[1] Rostovtzeff, *Orient and Greece.*

The political reforms included an extension of political rights to all citizens : all citizens were admitted to the popular assembly and were eligible as members of the jury in the law-courts. Thus nothing could become law without the consent of the whole citizen body and real equality of justice was established for the first time. But the magistracies were still restricted to those who were rich enough to serve in the cavalry. Solon was himself a landowner who had engaged in trade and belonged to one of the most noble families. His economic reforms put Athens on the road to commercial greatness and his political reforms paved the way for the achievement of true democracy.

Journalism and broadcasting were unknown ; to publish the principles behind his reforms Solon had recourse to poetry and wrote songs to be sung after dinner by the well-to-do. These songs would be sung again and again, and their vivid phrases, which often remind us of Hesiod, would stick in the memory and gradually create a public opinion ready to accept his legislation. In the long poem in which Solon described his ethical philosophy,[1] he developed an idea already present in Hesiod, and explained the apparent prosperity of the unrighteous and the suffering of the innocent by the theory that *hybris*—violence arising from pride in birth, wealth, strength, or intellect—once committed always gives rise to disaster, but the disaster may only befall the descendants of the sinner. This ethical theory is also the background of his political poems ; the following was clearly written before his archonship :

Our city [*polis*] will never incur ruin either from the apportionment of Zeus or by the will of the immortal gods :

[1] See my *Greek Interpretations*, 15 f. (M.U.P. 1942).

it is protected by Pallas Athene, great-souled guardian,
daughter of mighty Zeus. But the citizens themselves have
the will to destroy the great city in their folly. They listen
to gain and the rulers of the people have injustice in their
hearts ; for them awaits the suffering of many woes as a
result of mighty *hybris*. They cannot restrain their excesses
nor can they enjoy their good cheer in quiet and orderly
feasts. They are wealthy and listen to unjust deeds ; they
do not spare either sacred things or public things in their
thefts ; they do not keep in their hearts the holy foundations of justice [*dike*] : she is silent but knows the present
and the past, and at length she surely comes to punish.
This is a wound the whole city cannot escape, and it comes
swiftly to crippling slavery [rule by a tyrant], which
wakes from sleep intertribal strife and war, which destroys
the lovely youth of many. For swiftly foes waste away the
lovely town in meetings which favour the wrong-doers.
These evils range abroad among all the people ; of the
poor many come to other lands sold and bound with
shameful fetters. . . . So the public evil comes home to
each and the front gate can no longer keep it out but it
leaps over the high wall and finds you in the end even if
you have taken refuge in an innermost room. . . . These
things my soul bids me teach the Athenians, that most
evil comes to the city from Disorder, but Good Order
[*eunomia*] arranges all things well and fittingly and quickly
fetters the unjust, smooths the rough, stops excess, lames
hybris, withers the flowers of infatuation as they grow,
straightens crooked judgments, softens proud deeds, stops
the works of discord, stops the anger of bitter strife, makes
all things among men fitting and wise (fr. 3).

A short quotation must suffice from a poem written
by Solon after his law-giving when he no doubt felt
that he must justify himself to his fellow-nobles.

I gave the people [*demos*] as big a privilege as suffices,
neither taking from their privileges nor giving them more.

Those who had power and were respected for their wealth, these too I told to have no shameful gains. I stood with my strong shield over both and forbade to both an unjust victory. . . . So the people would follow best with their leaders if they are neither too free nor the victims of violence (fr. 5).

Though the solution left the poor little power and confirmed the rich in their right to executive magistracies, the rich had lost their right to enslave the poor and the poor had won a right to vote in the assembly and to sit on the jury in the law-courts ; this much was won by the nameless champions of the poor who made Solon's settlement both necessary and possible. Solon himself had set an example too rarely followed in Greek politics ; he had accepted extraordinary powers and had used them not only with great intelligence but also with complete disinterestedness. Twice again at moments of political crisis Athens produced men with the same qualities, Cleisthenes and Pericles.

III

"SOLON", says Professor Wade-Gery,[1] "left behind him a legacy of warring ambitions", and struggles, which we need not try to unravel, continued between the "men of the plain", i.e. the landed aristocracy, the "men of the shore", i.e. the merchants and artisans, and the "men of the hills", i.e. the smallholders and probably also the workers in the silver mines, who now found a champion in Peisistratus. About 560 B.C. Peisistratus, who had shown himself an extremely able general, seized the power and became tyrant of Athens. This was the "crippling slavery" which Solon had feared and threatened. Peisistratus' tyranny fell hardest on the aristocrats, many of whom were banished and their lands distributed among poor citizens; the poor citizens also benefited by his policy of public works, which included the demolition of the old city wall, the construction of an aqueduct, and the completion of a great temple to Athena Polias. The reorganisation of Athena's festival, the Panathenaea, as a great national festival, at which the *Iliad* and the *Odyssey* were recited, and the foundation of the City Dionysia, at which tragedy and comedy were performed in honour of Dionysus, made Athens the greatest cultural centre of Greece and stimulated the national consciousness; it is a practical justification of Solon's words already quoted : " [Our city] is protected by Pallas Athene, great-souled guardian, daughter of mighty Zeus." Peisistratus' foreign policy, which included alliances with Sparta and Argos and the establishment of Athenian influence on the

[1] *Classical Quarterly*, XXV, 78.

north-east coast of the Balkan peninsula, and on the shores of Macedonia, the Hellespont, and the Bosphorus (including the establishment of the elder Miltiades as tyrant of the Thracian Chersonese), helped the merchants by encouraging Athenian trade and ensuring supplies of imported corn, which made it possible to increase the urban population beyond the productive capacity of Attica itself.

After the death of Peisistratus in 528/7 B.C., the aristocrats and merchants again combined and with the help of Sparta, who was always prepared to champion the landed aristocracy, finally succeeded in expelling Peisistratus' son, the tyrant Hippias, who retired eventually to Persia to persuade the Great King to bring about his restoration. Cleisthenes, the leader of the merchants, "made friends with the people"; the aristocrats again called in Spartan assistance, but after a short occupation, the Spartans were expelled from the capital. Cleisthenes, who had already been archon in 525/4 B.C. in the time of Hippias, then began his reforms and gave Athens a new constitution, my account of which is in the main dependent on Rostovtzeff (*Orient and Greece*, 224 f.). Cleisthenes made the demes or parishes of Attica the chief electoral unit, and the franchise was conferred on every person registered as belonging to a deme. The demes were divided among three new areas ; the city—predominantly commercial and trading ; the coast—predominantly sailors, dockyard hands, and fishermen ; the plain of Attica with the hills—landholders large and small. The demes in these three areas were grouped in thirty *trittyes*, each containing several demes, ten *trittyes* to each area. The thirty *trittyes* in their turn were grouped in ten tribes in such a way that each tribe contained one *trittys* from each area. Thus, in each tribe, each class of the inhabitants was represented and the tribe became the basis of political and military organisation. The tribes each elected a military unit, commanded by an officer called the Strategos. The popular assembly voted by tribes, and the tribes elected the magistrates and the members of the judicial assembly. The new council of 500, also elected to represent the tribes, had control of foreign affairs and finance, besides the older function of preparing business for the Assembly (*ekklesia*). The magistrates were elected as before from the first two property classes only, i.e. from the well-to-do citizens. The practice of ostracism was probably also instituted by Cleisthenes : the assembly (consisting of a minimum quorum of 6,000) could vote by writing his name on potsherds (*ostraka*) that a prominent citizen should leave Athens for ten years, retaining, however, his rights and property ; this was clearly devised as a protection against tyranny and we shall note several occasions later on which it was used. The big step forward is clearly the new franchise arranged on a local basis, which meant that every citizen had a say in the election of the council, of the Strategoi, and of the other magistrates, just as he had a say in the legislative assembly and the judicature : in the Athenian national anthem, which was written in the first years of Cleisthenes' reforms, Athens is praised for its *isonomia*, " equality of laws ", the new democratic word which has supplanted Solon's *eunomia*, " Good Order ".

At the base of Cleisthenes' reforms lies a stronger belief in the political sense of the ordinary Athenian, a belief which must have been growing since the time of Solon. A reflection of the ideas of Athens during the later years of the Peisistratid tyranny has been seen in a drinking song written by the lyric poet

Simonides at the court of the tyrant Scopas of Thessaly, whither he went when Hippias was expelled from Athens. The poem (fr. 4) has been interpreted by Dr. C. M. Bowra in his *Greek Lyric Poetry* ; the text is preserved by Plato in his dialogue *Protagoras*.

It is hard for a man to be truly good, four-square in hands and feet and mind, wrought without a flaw. Pittacus' word does not seem to me consistent, though said by a wise man. He says it is difficult to be good. Only a god could have this praise ; a man cannot avoid being bad when impossible disaster overtakes him. Every man is good who fares well, every man is bad who fares ill. They, for the most part, are good whom the gods love. Therefore I will not waste a parcel of time on an empty impracticable hope, searching for what cannot happen, the completely blameless man, among all of us who eat the fruit of the broad-seated earth. But I have made a discovery and I will tell you. I commend and love all, whoever of his own free will does nothing ugly. With necessity not even the gods fight.

Dr. Bowra has shown that the emphasis on " free will " and the ethical meaning given to " ugly " are best paralleled in Athenian writers of the fifth century. Simonides means that the old saying of Pittacus " it is difficult to be good " does not make sense if you interpret " good " in the normal aristocratic sense of " prosperous " : prosperity does not depend on man but on the gods, and only the gods are good in this sense, because only the gods can claim freedom from misfortune. Simonides claims to have discovered that what matters is not beauty nor wits nor birth, not wealth but purity of motive, and this ideal may well have come to light in the liberal circles which, after the expulsion of Hippias, restored a new Athenian democracy ; it marks a revolution in Greek psychology from the time of Homer when Athena came from heaven and seized Achilles' golden hair and he changed his mind and put back his sword ; [1] the new democratic man is fully responsible for his actions. In the fragmentary last verse of the song, Simonides uses two other specifically Athenian ideas to describe his ideal man : " he knows the justice which blesses the city, a healthy man ". The " justice [*dike*] which blesses the city " is the Justice of which Solon spoke, and the political connotation of " healthy " is found again in fifth-century Athenian writers.

In this poem of Simonides the spirit behind the new democratic constitution of Cleisthenes takes shape for us almost as clearly as the spirit of Solon's reforms shines through his poems. For the other side of the picture, the spirit of the aristocratic landowners, who stood to lose by such reforms, the clearest exponents were Theognis of Megara in the sixth century and Pindar of Thebes in the fifth. Theognis of Megara wrote a series of songs in the form of admonitions to a younger man Cyrnus, which were sung at aristocrats' banquets and owe their preservation to their continued popularity among Athenian aristocrats in the fifth century. The following three poems show his views (53–68) :

Cyrnus, this city [*polis*] is still a city, but the people have changed. Who before knew neither lawsuits nor laws but lived with goatskins round their flanks and abode outside the city like deer, now they are good men, Cyrnus, and those who before were good are now useless. Who can endure this sight ? They cheat each other and laugh over each other for they do not know how to discriminate good from evil.

[1] Cf. *Greek Interpretations*, 5 f.

One of the causes of decay he found in mixed marriages
between the landed aristocracy and the merchant
class ; and here for the first time, when the supremacy
of the aristocracy was challenged, a Greek poet insisted
on purity of birth (an idea which later became the
foundation of Plato's state) (183 f., tr. T. F. Higham) :

Ram, ass, and horse, my Cyrnus, we look over
  with care, and seek good stock for good to cover ;
and yet the best men make no argument,
but wed, for money, runts of poor descent.
So too a woman will demean her state,
and spurn the better for the richer mate.
Money's the cry. Good stock to bad is wed
and bad to good, till all the world's cross-bred.
No wonder if the country's breed declines,—
mixed metal, Cyrnus, that but dimly shines.

It is perhaps even more interesting that in this restricted and unpleasant world, Theognis rose to a new
definition of virtue (*arete*). *Arete* is normally translated
virtue but means something more like excellence or
even efficiency. It need not, and often does not,
particularly in early Greek literature, refer to a moral
quality ; Homer for instance speaks of the *arete* of a
good runner's feet, and the *arete* of the Dorian noble
(as of the Homeric king) was military prowess.
Theognis now says (145–8, tr. Bowra) :

Choose, honouring the gods, to live in dearth,
  not to be rich with wealth unfairly won.
For in right doing [*dikaiosyne*] lies all good men's worth
  [*arete*] ;
  that man is good by whom the right is done.

Man's *arete* or virtue consists of *dikaiosyne*, a new word
signifying the quality of the *dikaios* or just man.
Hitherto, the word for justice has been *dike*, sometimes

c

believed to be a goddess and therefore a force in the external world. Now the new word separates off a kind of justice, which has nothing to do with the external world, but exists in the just man's heart and this quality is praised as the sum of all human good qualities.

Under constraint of necessity, the aristocrat has reached an ideal which is very near the ideal of Athenian democracy with its insistence on purity of motive. Although Pindar takes us into the fifth century, it is convenient to pursue the aristocratic ideal that much further here. Pindar wrote choral odes for the victors at the games which were held in the great religious festivals at Olympia and elsewhere. The competitors were mostly aristocrats, since only aristocrats had the leisure to train and the wealth to compete in these contests. Again and again Pindar stresses the ancestry of his victors, and in one ode he states the ideal (*Nem.* i, 37) : " It is right to walk in straight paths and fight according to one's breed "— the word translated " breed " (*physis*) means both " process of growth " and also the character begotten in a man by his father. In another ode he says (*Nem.* iii, 70) : " Inborn valour gives a man full power ; he who depends on learning is in darkness, swayed by winds, comes into the lists with unfirm feet, tastes countless forms of prowess without the will to completion." To this belief in breed, Pindar adds piety (*eusebeia*, the belief in the omnipotence and beneficence of the gods), modesty, and chivalry (*Pyth.* xix, 95—" he bade him praise even his foe if he acted justly with all his heart "). I have adopted modesty as the standard translation for the Greek word *sophrosyne* because I think it gives its flavour better than anything else. *Sophrosyne* as it is used in the fifth century is the opposite of *hybris*. *Hybris* means letting your wealth, power, strength, or skill lead you astray into committing acts of arrogance or violence ; if you have *sophrosyne*, you remember that you are mortal and that all these excesses are dangerous and perishable ; therefore in word and deed you always keep within the bounds that are appointed for a mortal—you are uncomplaining in disaster and modest in success. Breed, piety, and modesty are the leading ideas of the Athenian aristocrats who were Pindar's friends and among his employers, and we shall see in due course how they are opposed by the aristocrats to the democratic ideal of Pericles.

IV

BOTH tragedy and comedy were performed at the annual festival of Dionysus which was instituted by Peisistratus, and the audience was the whole citizen body. At each festival three tragic and three comic poets were chosen to produce plays in competition for prizes, and a rich citizen was chosen to produce for each of the poets. We have some evidence that Aeschylus was the poet of the democrats and Sophocles the poet of the aristocrats in the fact that in 468 B.C., when the board of Strategoi judged the tragedies instead of the ordinary board of judges, the aristocratic leader Cimon awarded the prize to the youthful Sophocles instead of to the mature Aeschylus ; and four years before in 472 B.C. Aeschylus' *Persae* was produced by Pericles, the coming democratic leader. The plays were produced at a religious festival and represented (with rare exceptions, of which the *Persae* is one) the great figures of the heroic age ; no attempt was made at historical accuracy, but the heroic legends were used as a vehicle for the ideas and ideals of fifth-century Athens. Two things distinguish Athenian dramatic poetry from any preceding poetry : the audience was 13,000 including women, children, and foreigners, not a group such as the king's court or the nobles' friends, and the dramatic form was admirably suited for representing the clash of personalities and the question of purity of motive, raised at the end of the sixth century by the poem of Simonides.

Aeschylus was born in 525 and died in 456 B.C. The major external event during these fifty years was the Persian War. When the Persian Empire had been extended in the late sixth century to include the Greek cities of the Asia Minor coast, the next step was to attack Greece itself, because the conquest of Asia Minor had inevitably drawn the Persians into European politics. In 493 B.C. two new figures appeared in Athens, Themistocles and the younger Miltiades. Themistocles was of obscure origin and has probably been rightly described as " the first political leader at Athens who did not belong to one of the old noble families ". He was elected archon in 493 B.C. and was responsible for permitting the production of Phrynichus' *Capture of Miletus*, a tragedy designed to bring home to the Athenians the horrors of the Ionian revolt against Persia in 499 B.C., and therefore the advisability of preparing against a similar fate themselves. Miltiades was an Athenian aristocrat, who had been made tyrant of the Thracian Chersonese by the Peisistratids and now returned to Athens, ejected by the Persian king Darius. He convinced the Athenians that resistance to Persia was possible with the help of Sparta and carried this policy through ; Themistocles presumably also saw the necessity of Spartan aid.

In 492 B.C. Darius struck along the northern shores of the Aegean but his fleet was wrecked off Mt. Athos. In 490 B.C. Darius was ready again and this time avowed his intention of capturing Athens. The Persians landed on the plain of Marathon and were decisively defeated by Miltiades ; Aeschylus was among those who fought. The next ten years were occupied by preparations on both sides. The string of ostracisms in Athens are evidence of the power of the popular leader Themistocles, and in 487 B.C. for the first time the nine archons, who had hitherto always been elected, were selected by lot from fifty men elected from each tribe by the demesmen ; the result was that the archonship became more democratic but sank in importance relatively to the office of Strategos, which continued to be elective. In 483 B.C. the Laureion silver mines produced a surplus of 200 talents and it was proposed to share this out among the citizens, 10 drachmae (ten days' wages) apiece ; Themistocles carried through a counter-proposal to build a fleet of 200 ships immediately against Aegina but ultimately against Persia.

The Persians struck again under Xerxes and Mardonius in 480 B.C. and met a united Greece ; the exiles had been recalled to Athens. As in the Marathon campaign, the Spartans were unwilling to leave the Peloponnese in any force and the contingent they sent to Thermopylae was inadequate to hold the pass. Attica was invaded but the Athenians won so decisive a victory at Salamis that Xerxes retired to Persia, leaving a powerful army with Mardonius in Thessaly. This army again invaded Attica in 479 B.C. and was decisively defeated by the Spartans at Plataea ; this battle and a naval defeat at Mycale on the other side of the Aegean ended for the present the Persian menace to Greece.

But the Greek cities in Asia Minor still had to be freed. Sparta proposed unpractically that the Greeks in Asia Minor should be settled on the lands of those cities in Greece which had given in to the Persians, and Sparta in any case was land-bound. Athens took the lead ; Themistocles rebuilt the fortifications of Athens in spite of Spartan opposition—he undoubtedly saw that the danger for Athenian democracy no longer came from Persia but from Sparta. Xanthippus (the father of Pericles), Cimon (the son of Miltiades), and Aristides pushed the war eastwards. In 477 B.C. Aristides organised the Delian League of the allies with a common council and treasury in Apollo's sacred island of Delos. Little was heard of Themistocles in these years except that in 476 B.C. he acted as producer to Phrynichus' *Phoenician Women*, a tragedy on the Persian Wars. The conservatives were probably mobilising their forces against him ; we know from several sources that the Council of the Areopagus, which had been the Council of the Kings and still had a strongly aristocratic flavour, regained its power after the Persian Wars and according to Aristotle " directed the city " (*Athp.* 23). With many of the young men away at the wars, this conservative body could block democratic progress ; in particular Themistocles' anti-Spartan policy was directly contrary to their wishes, since like all Greek aristocrats they believed their salvation lay in close alliance with Sparta. They managed to get Themistocles ostracised in 471 B.C. ; he went to Argos where he intrigued against Sparta.

The year before Themistocles was ostracised Pericles produced Aeschylus' *Persae* at the Dionysiac festival. How far Aeschylus' play was indebted to the earlier play of Phrynichus, the *Phoenician Women*, we cannot say because we know too little about the *Phoenician Women*. Aeschylus laid the scene in Persia and drew from the story of the Persian defeat the characteristically Athenian moral that Xerxes' defeat was due to *hybris*, the *hybris* of trying to conquer by sea when fate had decreed that Persia should be a land power. King Darius, who is summoned from his tomb to give advice to the Persian elders after they have heard the news of Salamis, so phrases it when he has given them warning of the coming disaster of Plataea (816 f., tr. Murray) :

An oozing crust Plataea's field shall know
of mire blood-soaked beneath the Dorian lance ;
and piles of dead dumb warning shall advance
even to our children's children, that the eye
of mortal man lift not his hopes too high.
Pride [*hybris*] in her flower makes full the barren ears
of *Ate*, and no harvest hath but tears.

The story of Plataea as told by Aeschylus makes the
single brief reference to Sparta quoted above—
" beneath the Dorian lance "—and no word is wasted
on the Spartan heroes who fought at Thermopylae
and have captured the world's imagination ever since.
The centrepiece of the play is the story of Salamis
and the credit is given to Themistocles, because Xerxes
gave battle at Salamis on the strength of a message
from Themistocles that the Greeks were going to try
to escape.   When the Persian queen Atossa asks who
began the battle, the messenger answers (353, tr.
Murray) :

Queen, for the first beginning of these woes,
some fiend or madman—whence he came, who knows ?—
Greek seeming, from the Athenian ranks drew near
to Xerxes' self, and whispered in his ear
that, once the veil of hiding night should fall,
the Greeks would wait no more.

No one could mistake here the allusion to Themistocles,
placed at the head of the account of Salamis.   The
shorter pendant story of the mopping up on Psyttaleia
is told without any allusion to Aristides, who according to Herodotus was responsible for this incident.
One other allusion would make the audience think
of Themistocles : when Atossa asks the chorus what
wealth the Athenians have, the chorus answers :
" a silver fountain-spring is theirs, a secret treasure-

house of earth "—a clear allusion to the use of the surplus from the silver-mines to build the ships for Salamis. The whole passage is worth reading (231 f., tr. Murray):

Atossa. Say where, in all this peopled world, a city men call Athens lies?

Leader. Far distant, where our Lord the Sun sinks and his last effulgence dies.

Atossa. And this far western land it is my son so craved to make his prey?

Leader. Aye, for if Athens once were his, all Hellas must his word obey.

Atossa. Has Athens then such multitudes, such hosts of mighty men to lead?

Leader. A faithful army, which of old hath wrought much havoc on the Mede.

Atossa. An army; have they likewise wealth, enough to keep the land from dearth?

Leader. A silver fountain-spring is theirs, a secret treasure-house of earth.

Atossa. What weapon flashes in their hands? Have they the bow that smites afar?

Leader. Not so; the spear that stabbeth close, the shield that goes not back in war.

Atossa. What master holds them in the fray, what shepherd's rod to drive the herd?

Leader. To no man living are they slaves, nor bow them before no man's word.

Atossa. Unmastered, how can they endure the onset of an angry foe?

Leader. Methinks Darius knoweth, and his great and goodly armies know.

Thus Aeschylus' answer to the question, Who won the Persian Wars?, given the year before Themistocles' eclipse, is quite clear; the Persian Wars were won by the Athenian democracy with the help of the gods and the genius of Themistocles, and this answer would no doubt also have been given by the producer, the young democratic politician Pericles, the son of Xanthippus, who married Cleisthenes' niece.

Meanwhile the war in the East had been continued, but with Cimon's victory over the Persians at the river Eurymedon in 468 B.C. the Persians were left with no marine base north of the coast of Palestine. (It was in this year that Cimon awarded the tragic prize to Sophocles in preference to Aeschylus.) The allies in the confederation of Delos felt that their work was done and wanted to leave the confederacy. Naxos had revolted in 469 and Thasos revolted in 465 B.C. Rostovtzeff points out that Athens had two alternatives —" either to renounce the mastery of the Aegean and to revert to the state of things before the Persian Wars, or to convert the Federation into an Athenian Empire " ; [1] in other words to rule the allies instead of presiding over them, a result which could only be secured by force. She was induced to take the second of these courses, partly by her conviction that the struggle with Persia was not yet over, and partly by other considerations. Athens had become a great city : a large part of the Aegean trade was concentrated there ; and she had become an important centre of industry. The population had greatly increased : to the citizens were added a multitude of aliens (*metoikoi*) who did not possess the franchise but settled in the city to carry on trade and industry ; the number of slaves had also risen greatly. The loss of mastery over the sea would certainly have arrested this development ; and it might also have forced on Athens a return to the conditions that existed before the Persian Wars ; and such a return would inevitably have brought with it

[1] *Orient and Greece*, 366.

serious internal convulsions. Hence she chose the second course and proceeded to convert the federation into an empire, in which the citizens of Athens ruled over the citizens of other states, and the contributions of the allies became tribute instead. This policy was already implied in the suppression of the revolts in Naxos and Thasos ; its chief offensive effort was the expedition against Egypt in 461 B.C. which was designed to strike a blow at the southernmost extremity of the Persian Empire. The democrats saw that it was the only method of securing both the corn from the Black Sea, which was necessary to support the increased population of Athens, and the tribute from the empire, which made the complete democracy of the later fifth century possible.

Between 465 and 460 B.C. Pericles and the democrats achieved power. In 464 B.C. an earthquake occurred in Sparta and the Spartan slaves (the Helots) took their chance to revolt. The Spartans asked for Athenian help and Cimon took a force of 4,000 heavy armed troops. In the absence of Cimon and so many of his supporters, the democrats struck. The next year is noted by Aristotle as the end of the domination of the Areopagus (*Athp.* 25) :

as the proletariat became more powerful [he is thinking particularly of the poorer citizens in the navy, who were now becoming vocal] Ephialtes, the son of Sophonides, who was champion of the people and seemed to be both incorruptible and a good constitutionalist, attacked the council [of the Areopagus], and first he removed many of the councillors by prosecuting them for their official acts and then in 461 B.C. he took away all their accretions of power by which they had become guardians of the constitution, and gave these functions back partly to the Council of 500, partly to the people and to the law-courts.

The Areopagus' sole remaining function, which it had possessed from the beginning, was to be a murder court. Ephialtes was aided by the change in the character of the Areopagus itself, since the archons ceased to be elected : [1]

from 487 onwards, the archons are nobodies : this has not sensibly diluted the Areopagus by 480, but the process is still cumulative : by 461 there were probably few, if any, elected archons still sitting in the council : its hollow prestige is smashed by Ephialtes. A change in the personnel of the archons means a change in the Areopagus, but it takes nearly 30 years for the change to become complete.

Shortly afterwards Ephialtes was murdered, which left Pericles to lead the democrats.

Cimon's expedition had been sent home by the Spartans, who were apparently frightened that the Athenians with their democratic sympathies would be won over by the Helots and turn against the Spartans themselves (Thuc. I, 102/3). This was a heavy blow to the prestige of the conservatives. The Athenians ostracised Cimon on his return in 462 B.C. and made an alliance with Argos with the intention of setting up a strong and friendly buffer state in the North Peloponnese between themselves and Sparta ; although the Spartans and the Athenian aristocrats had succeeded in hounding Themistocles out of Argos in 468 B.C. this alliance represents the fruits of his sojourn there and a return to his policy.

This is the internal and external background of the *Oresteia*, which Aeschylus wrote for the festival in 458 B.C. In the three successive plays he dramatised the story of the murder of Agamemnon by his wife Clytaemnestra, the murder of Clytaemnestra by their

[1] Wade-Gery, *Classical Quarterly*, XXV, 81.

son Orestes, and the trial and acquittal of Orestes by
the Athenian court of the Areopagus.   There are two
moments in this great trilogy which concern us ; one
is Agamemnon's decision to kill his daughter Iphigenia
and the other is the political references of the last play,
the *Eumenides*. The earlier moment is of interest to
us here because it shows that Aeschylus would have
answered with Simonides that the good man is the
man whose motive is pure.   However hardly the scales
were weighted against Agamemnon because he was
commander-in-chief of the Greek army, he was responsible for his own ruin ; by sacrificing Iphigenia he
committed the initial act of *hybris* which involved him
in *ate* (infatuation) ; like Xerxes in the *Persae* he
started the disastrous train of events.[1]

Professor Tierney [2] has pointed out that Aeschylus
showed his approval of the Argive alliance by transfer-
ring the setting of the story to Argos.   In Homer (as
later in Sophocles) Agamemnon was killed at Mycenae ;
according to Stesichorus the murder took place in
Sparta and Pindar adopts this form of the myth in
Pythian, XI, which he wrote in 454 for a Theban victor,
as a conscious criticism of Aeschylus.[3]   Aeschylus'
second great innovation was to make the trial of
Orestes take place in Athens ; in other versions Orestes
was purified in Delphi and that was the end : by
these innovations the new Argive alliance could be
given its mythical sanction.   Orestes reaching Athens
makes this prayer to Athena (*Eum*. 287 f., tr. Murray) :

> And now, with lips of grace,
> Once more I pray the lady of this place,
> Athena, to mine aid. Let her but come ;
> Myself, mine Argive people, and my home

[1] See further *Greek Interpretations*, 42.   [2] *Studies*, 1938, 93 f.
[3] Bowra, *Classical Quarterly*, XXX, 129.

> Shall without war be hers, hers true of heart
> And changeless. Therefore wheresoe'er thou art,
> In some far wilderness of Libyan earth,
> By those Tritonid waters of thy birth ;
> Upgirt for deeds or veilèd on thy throne ;
> Or is it Phlegra's field thou broodst upon,
> Guiding the tempest, like some Lord of War ?
> Oh hear ! A goddess heareth though afar.

Aeschylus not only gives the mythical sanction for the Argive alliance but, by summoning Athena from Libya where the Egyptian expedition was taking place and from Phlegra in the far North where the Athenians were active in Chalcidice, he refers to the forward external policy of the democrats.

Their home policy also influenced the end of the *Eumenides*. As a murderer, Orestes is tried before the Areopagus and this council is also given its mythical sanction as a murder court, but *not* as the government of Athens : Aeschylus is on the side of Pericles and Ephialtes. Athena's speech establishes the Areopagus as a murder court, but gives it the prestige and majesty due to its long history : " this council which no thought of gain can touch, revered, swift to wrath, a wakeful guard over sleepers " (704).

Orestes is acquitted by the court of the Areopagus but the play does not end here. A long dialogue between Athena and his accusers, the Eumenides, the avenging spirits of his mother Clytaemnestra, ends in their establishment as friends of Athens in a cave under the Areopagus, to which they are formally conducted in torchlight procession by the citizens of Athens. Why so much trouble ? Partly, of course, to give the newly established murder court the sanction of the old avenging spirits of a less civilised order. But Sir

Richard Livingstone [1] has made a good case for seeing in the wrath of the Eumenides an allegorisation of the bitter passions of the defeated conservatives and in their reconciliation a plea to the conservatives to be reconciled to the Athenian democracy. As the play goes on, the particular and gruesome aspect of the Eumenides ("Women? Nay, never women, Gorgon shapes of yore . . . all shadows, black abominable. The voices of their slumber rise and swell, back-beating, and their eyes drop gouts of gore" (47, tr. Murray) is forgotten, and the gist of their argument is that of defenders of the Areopagus :

There is a place where fear is well and should be enthroned to watch hearts. Modesty in a little room brings profit. But what man or city, whose heart is not reared in the light, would reverence justice ? Do not praise life without government or life under a tyrant. God gives victory to moderation—for the rest he has other aims. In harmony I say : *hybris* is the true child of impiety, but from health of heart comes wealth, which is kind to all and most desired. In sum I say : reverence the altar of justice. Do not kick it away with godless foot because you see gain. For vengeance will come ; the end is fixed (517–42).

It is clear that their words are not only closely allied to Athena's proclamation, but have earlier echoes— Simonides' "health of heart" from the Cleisthenic period and earlier still, Solon's Justice, his view that the people must be "neither too free nor the victims of violence", his praise of god-given wealth, and his condemnation of ill-gotten gain. This is traditional Athenian thought and the Eumenides are speaking in the terms that might well be used by the conservative defenders of the Areopagus. Aeschylus himself deeply

[1] *Journal of Hellenic Studies*, 1925, 120 f.

sympathised with it and feared that Athens might lose something extremely precious if the bitterness of party politics expelled the upholders of these traditions.

When the verdict has been given for Orestes, Athena persuades them to stay in Athens : one phrase in particular shows that Aeschylus is thinking here not of the Eumenides but of the conservatives (851) : " if you go to a foreign shore, you will still be in love with Athens ". It was Pericles who later called the Athenians " lovers of their city ". So Aeschylus in the *Eumenides* is pleading for reconciliation between the contending parties because both sides are " in love with Athens ".

V

PERICLES, PROTAGORAS, AND SOPHOCLES

THE thirty-odd years from 460 B.C. to 429 B.C. are called the age of Pericles, because Pericles' genius dominates Athenian policy during this period, which ends with his death. In these thirty years the Athenian empire reached both its greatest expansion and its most efficient organisation. The tribute paid by the city-states within the empire in return for Athenian protection of the Aegean enabled Pericles to realise full democracy by providing much employment and payment for much state service. At the same time he was able to put forward another justification for the Athenian empire : Athens was to become a centre of Greek civilisation, " an education for Hellas ".

In 460 B.C. Athens had already embarked on the Egyptian expedition and had just made alliances with Argos and Thessaly as part of the new anti-Spartan programme ; the decision to convert the Delian confederacy into an Athenian empire had already been taken. The final failure of the Egyptian expedition in 456–454 and a barren victory in Cyprus in 450 B.C., won by Cimon, who had returned from exile and died during the campaign, led to final peace with Persia in 448 B.C. At the same time Athens was involved in the First Peloponnesian War with Aegina, Corinth, Boeotia, and ultimately with Sparta.

Aegina was an old enemy and a rival. Corinth with her western allies excluded Athens from the Italian coast and the great grain-markets of Italy and Sicily . . . Italy and Sicily could supply both her needs (raw material and food-stuffs) more fully than any country except Egypt . . . To Sparta (and to all Peloponnesians) the neutrality of the

Isthmus was of vital importance, because they depended largely on the import of corn and raw material from Italy and Sicily.[1]

After great initial successes Athens' only lasting gain was to have made Aegina part of her empire and Pericles was forced to conclude a thirty-years' peace with Sparta in 446 B.C. and for the moment to accept again the Athens-Sparta dualism beloved of the aristocrats. Two further attempts to expand westwards were made : in 446 the ancient South Italian town of Sybaris invited the Athenians to help them refound their city and the Athenians ultimately sent out a new colony in 444–443 to a new city, Thurii, in the neighbourhood.[2] Secondly, in 433 B.C. Pericles made an alliance with Corcyra, which was a colony of Corinth and a very important stage on the route to the west. It is interesting to note that in both cases he may have been following out the policy of Themistocles, who is described as a " benefactor of Corcyra " and had called one of his daughters Sybaris. The alliance with Corcyra which aimed at strangling Corinth's western trade led directly to the Second Peloponnesian War.

Meanwhile the conversion of the Delian confederacy into an Athenian empire had continued. The treasury of the league was transferred to Athens from Delos in 454 B.C. The great majority of the so-called allies now paid tribute to Athens and were obliged to refer important lawsuits to Athens.[3] Athens also intervened to support the local democratic party against the oligarchy. Athenians were also settled on allied territory in " cleruchies ", which were not independent colonies

[1] Rostovtzeff, *Orient and Greece*, 269.

[2] See for details Wade-Gery, *Journal of Hellenic Studies*, 1932, 217 f.

[3] Cf. Thuc. I., 77, examined by Hopper in *Journal of Hellenic Studies*, 1943, 35.

with a loose tie to the mother-city but pieces of Athens abroad and had the double aim of relieving over-population in Athens and of garrisoning the empire, e.g. Aegina, Euboea, Naxos, Lemnos, Imbros, and the Chersonese.[1] Serious revolts which needed major expeditions to quell them were made by Euboea in 446 B.C. and Samos in 440 B.C.

The complement of this external policy was Pericles' internal policy of rebuilding Athens to make her worthy of her new position as an imperial city. The funds for this rebuilding were provided from the tribute of the allies. Pericles had two intentions : one was to employ the maximum of citizens on public works, the other was to provide " an education for Greece ". In his *Life of Pericles* Plutarch says that the whole city received pay from the state ; the building programme provided state-paid work for all the various kinds of craftsmen and labourers employed on it, just as the army and the navy, the garrisons, the expeditions, and the embassies provided state employment for those who were the right age and had the right qualifications to perform these duties. At the same time, Pericles instituted payment for state services : for service in the law-courts (Aristotle, *Athp.* 27/4), the Council of 500, and possibly also for attendance at the theatre. This made it possible for the poorest citizen to take the necessary time off to perform state service. The archonship was thrown open to the third class of citizens (those whose yearly income was 200 bushels of corn and above) in 457 B.C.

Pericles had also an educational aim and knew what kind of citizen he needed to run his democracy. The clearest expression of this is in the Funeral Oration,

---

[1] Cf. for the details of the growth of imperialism in the fifties, Meiggs, *Journal of Hellenic Studies*, 1943, 21.

which Pericles delivered in 431 B.C. over those who had been killed in the first year of the Second Peloponnesian war : the historian Thucydides heard the speech and certainly recorded the spirit, if not the actual words, of what Pericles said. The following extracts are adapted from Jowett's translation (Thuc. II, 37/1) :

We are called a democracy because the administration is in the hands of the many and not of the few. But while the law secures equal justice to all alike in their private disputes, the claim of excellence is also recognised ; and when a citizen is in any way distinguished, he is preferred to the public service, not as a matter of privilege, but as the reward of merit [*arete*]. Neither is poverty a bar, but a man may benefit his country whatever may be the obscurity of his condition. . . . [37/3] While we are thus unconstrained in our private intercourse, a spirit of reverence pervades our public acts ; we are prevented from doing wrong by respect for authority and for the laws, having an especial regard to those which are ordained for the protection of the injured as well as to those unwritten laws which bring upon the transgressor of them the reprobation of the general sentiment.

In these passages Pericles claims the essential equalities of democracy, equality of justice or equality before the law (*isonomia* in its specifically Athenian sense, as used in the Athenian national anthem), equality of opportunity, which does not mean that every man has a right to everything but that rewards in official life depend upon *arete* or excellence and not on birth or wealth, and finally social equality, respect for the conscience and for idiosyncrasies of private behaviour. At the same time he faces the problem of excessive individualism and claims that cohesion is maintained in the Athenian state by respect for its written and unwritten traditions. Here Pericles is very near the words of

Athena in Aeschylus' *Eumenides* (698 f.) : " do not cast
all fear outside the city. What man is just who has
no fear ? " Nothing in these sentiments, which are
in the straight tradition of Athenian thought, would be
rejected by the aristocrats, and Pericles is in fact
demanding in his citizens *sophrosyne*, the aristocratic
virtue of modesty described above ; *sophrosyne* is also
the message of the sculpture on the great new temple
of Athena, the Parthenon, since much of the sculpture
represents mythical battles which were for the fifth
century Athenian symbols of the triumph of *sophrosyne*
over *hybris*.[1] Nor would the aristocrats disagree with
the famous sentence (40/1) " We are lovers of the
beautiful without extravagance, and we cultivate the
mind without loss of manliness."

But the following paragraph states the new democratic ideal of *polypragmosyne* (meddling), as its opponents called it, against the aristocratic ideal of *apragmosyne* (the carefree life of cultured ease, an idea which
had already appeared in Solon's time and then again
in the reduced desires and pretensions of Theognis'
aristocrats, and in the fifth century is becoming something very like escapism) (40/2) :

An Athenian citizen does not neglect the state because
he takes care of his own household ; and even those of us
who are engaged in business have a very fair idea of politics.
We alone regard a man who takes no interest in public
affairs not as a harmless [*apragmon*], but as a useless character ; and if few of us are originators, we are all sound
judges of a policy. . . . [41/1] To sum up, I say that
Athens is the school of Hellas and that the individual
Athenian in his own person seems to have the power of
adapting himself to the most varied forms of action with
the utmost versatility and grace.

[1] See *Greek Interpretations*, 54.

We know a good deal about the struggle that it cost Pericles to put his policy through. The ideals of the aristocratic party were piety, modesty, cultured ease (*apragmosyne*), and the privileges of breed (*physis*). They were prepared to fight Persians who were barbarians, i.e. not Greek, but they believed in friendship with Sparta and a Greek world of equal states in which cultured men such as themselves could freely intermingle at the great Hellenic festivals. Plutarch (*Life of Pericles*, 12) quotes a contemporary speech on the building programme which describes it as " violence [*hybris*] to Hellas and open tyranny when we gild and beautify Athens like a pretentious woman, hanging round her neck jewels and statues and thousand talent temples ". Some idea of their influence in voting power at the Assembly can be gathered from Aristotle, who says (*Athp.* 27/3) that Pericles instituted the payment for jurors as a means of winning votes from Cimon :

For Cimon, who had princely wealth, both performed public services [such as producing tragedies] in a princely manner and supported many of the demesmen. For any of the Lakiadai on any day could come and get his due from him, and his estates were all unfenced so that anyone who liked could pick his fruit.

When Cimon was ostracised the leadership of the aristocratic party passed to Thucydides, not the historian but the son of Melesias, who had an international reputation in aristocratic circles as a wrestler and a trainer of wrestlers. This feudal method of catching votes was not enough for Thucydides but according to Plutarch (*Life of Pericles*, 11)

he would not suffer those who were called the honest and good to be scattered up and down and mix themselves and be lost among the populace, as formerly, diminishing and obscuring their superiority amongst the mass ; but taking them apart by themselves and uniting them in one body, by their combined weight he was able, as it were upon the balance, to make a counterpoise to the other party.

Professor Wade-Gery [1] comments :

The Opposition was instructed to vote, not on the merits of the case, but as it bore on the question of breaking Pericles ; not by their private judgment but as the party decreed. The party, a state within the state, sat as one body on the Pnyx.

The opposition apparently came to some sort of a head in 445 B.C. when the first Peloponnesian War had ended in a rather unsatisfactory peace and the war with Persia was also over. In the spring of 444 B.C., Pericles (for the last time in his life) failed to be elected Strategos. Next spring Thucydides himself was ostracised and Pericles did not suffer from him for ten years ; soon after his return in 433 B.C. he began a series of vexatious prosecutions against Pericles' friends.

After the ostracism of Thucydides, Pericles was Strategos for fifteen years consecutively until he died in 429 B.C. Summing up the whole period of Pericles' domination in Athenian politics, Thucydides the historian (II, 65, Jowett) says that

Pericles, deriving authority from his capacity and acknowledged worth, being also a man of transparent integrity, was able to control the multitude in a free spirit ; he led them rather than was led by them ; for, not seeking power by dishonest arts, he had no need to say pleasant things, but on the strength of his own high character could venture to oppose and even to anger them. When he saw them unseasonably elated and arrogant [*hybris*], his words

[1] *Journal of Hellenic Studies*, 1932, 208.

humbled and awed them, and when they were depressed by groundless fears he sought to reanimate their confidence. Thus Athens, though still in name a democracy, was in fact ruled by her greatest citizen.

Although the constitutional history of Athens, as we have tried to sketch it, is the history of the gradual growth of democratic institutions, viewed from another standpoint it could be regarded as the history of great men—Solon, Peisistratus, Cleisthenes, Themistocles, and Pericles. All except Themistocles came from noble families of considerable or great wealth, and Themistocles' position had been, as we have seen, precarious and subject to frequent interruption by the aristocratic opposition. The ascendancy of Solon, Peisistratus, and Cleisthenes was abnormal and due to special crises. Pericles' position, however, was constitutional; he was re-elected year after year as Strategos, and he owed his ascendancy, as Thucydides says, to his genius and to his integrity; but his continued ascendancy caused the constitutional anomaly that Athens, " though still in name a democracy, was in fact ruled by her greatest citizen ".

The interest of Thucydides' account lies not only in its statement of fact but also in its awareness of a new constitutional development. The Athenians were now not only interested in political practice but also in political theory. The rise of democracy in Athens gave birth to the political thinker. " The average citizen sought guidance and felt the necessity of political education : he was often conscious of his own helplessness." [1] Thucydides' account was not written before the end of the fifth century, but we have other evidence, as Professor Morrison [2] has shown, that the theory of

[1] Rostovtzeff, *Orient and Greece*, 296.
[2] *Classical Quarterly*, XXXV, 1 f.

Periclean " monarchy " was invented much earlier by the thinker Protagoras, who was closely associated with Pericles. The evidence comes from Plato and from Herodotus. In the dialogue *Theaetetus* (167) Plato makes Protagoras defend his thesis that man is the measure of all things : in the course of this defence Protagoras says :

wise and good orators substitute in their cities sound for unsound views of what is right. For whatever seems right and honourable to each city, is so for it so long as it holds by them. Only, when anything is in any particular case unsound for them, the wise man substitutes something else that is and appears sound.

This conception that the duty of the statesman is to form public opinion by his own judgment comes close to the Thucydidean portrait of Pericles, and it is therefore reasonable to suppose that Plato has recorded a genuine memory of Protagoras. Another genuine memory of Protagoras is recorded by the historian Herodotus, who evidently drew deeply on Athenian thought during his stay in Athens and largely remodelled his history of the relations between Greece and the East under the influence of ideas current in Athens. Writing between 448 and 442 B.C., at a time when Protagoras was in Athens and the Periclean ascendancy needed justification, he represented monarchy as an alternative theory of government beside tyranny, democracy, and oligarchy (III, 80–2) : monarchy is the rule of the best man, who, being best in intellectual ability, " would act blamelessly as the steward of the people ". Here again we are very near both to the " wise and good orator " of Protagoras and to the Thucydidean portrait of Pericles.

Herodotus was ostensibly writing an account of how

the Persians decided on the best form of government in 520 B.C., but it is far more likely that the discussion reflects political theorising at Athens where he was writing during the contest for power between Thucydides, son of Melesias, and Pericles. The disadvantage of tyranny is that it is subject to no audit ; even the best man in such a position " would stand outside the normal run of thoughts ", for he is prone both to violence (*hybris*) and to jealousy. The final summing up is that tyrants " disturb traditional laws, rape women, and put men to death without trial ", whereas " democracy has the fair name of Equality " (*isonomia* —the democratic word for equality of justice as opposed to *eunomia*, good order, which has now become an aristocratic word) ; " magistrates are chosen by lot, magistrates are subject to audit, all policy is discussed in public " ; this is an adequate description of democracy under Pericles, as it was in theory. The champion of oligarchy counters that nothing is more unintelligent or more violent (*hybris*) than the good-for-nothing mob. The tyrant at least knows what he is doing ; the mob has no knowledge : " how should it know when it has neither been taught nor knows anything good of its own ". The sense here is that the aristocrat has traditional standards ; Pindar would attribute them to birth, but Protagoras [1] rationalises and says that the sons of the rich are the best educated because they go to school earlier than anyone else and leave it later.

The mob [continues the Herodotean champion of oligarchy] falls on problems and sweeps them along senselessly like a river in spate . . . we will choose a company of the best men and invest them with the power : for we

[1] Plato, *Protagoras*, 326c.

ourselves shall be of this number and the decisions of the best men are naturally the best.

Professor Morrison rightly calls this " the selfish and bigoted point of view of an aristocracy in retreat ". The champion of monarchy answers that oligarchy causes rivalries between leading men which give rise to civil war, murder, and so to monarchy ; democracy leads to parties within the state who combine to rob the state for their private gain, until some champion of the people arises to stop them : " he wins the admiration of the people and hey ! presto ! he is a monarch ".

This discussion recorded by Herodotus shows how far the Greeks had gone in the forties of the fifth century in formulating the characteristics of the different constitutions known to them and many of the formulations are echoed by later writers such as Plato. The monarch, carefully distinguished from the unconstitutional tyrant, is the peg on which Herodotus hangs the whole discussion because the King of Persia was constitutional in a way in which the Greek tyrant never was ; Pericles' continual re-election as Strategos gave him a somewhat similar constitutional position. Once conceived in these terms, the idea of the responsible expert as sole governor of the state developed in due course into Plato's philosopher king and Isocrates' educated monarch.

Apart from the special position of Pericles himself, Protagoras justified the democratic belief in the amateur judgment. In the Platonic dialogue named after him (322d–e) he maintains that the foundations of political virtue are Justice (*dikaiosyne*) and Modesty ; these are virtues which everyone can be expected to possess and therefore the Athenians " have good reason for admit-

ting a smith's or a cobbler's counsel in public affairs "
(324c). He goes on to consider how they gain these
essential virtues ; his answer is the normal process of
education—nurse, mother, tutor, school, and finally
(326c)

the city compels them to learn the laws and live by these
as a model that they may not act capriciously of their own
free will . . . but the city gives them the laws which were
invented by old and good lawgivers as a blue-print by which
both to act in office and to accept official rulings, and
constrains anyone who goes outside them ; the name of
this constraint in Athens and many other cities is *euthyna*
because justice straightens them.

Thus the old Hesiodic idea of a " straight decision "
is taken over into the Athenian conception of an audit
at the end of a magistracy, and law (*nomos*) is the
greatest political educative force.

Another political document of these years is
Sophocles' *Antigone*, which was produced either in
443 B.C. or in 441 B.C. Sophocles' political alignment
was with the friends of Cimon, and if the play was
produced in the spring of 443 B.C., it must have been
written in 444 B.C., the year of Pericles' eclipse.
Sophocles may have been thinking of Pericles when he
drew the figure of Creon : he gives Creon Pericles'
title of Strategos and once makes him use a phrase
which Thucydides later puts into the mouth of Pericles :
" nor would I ever count the country's foe my friend
knowing this, that the city is our salvation and we
can only make our friends if she sails upright " (186 f.,
cf. Thuc. II, 60). The conservative cannot conceive
that a democratic politician, who had achieved a
unique position, could possibly fail to take advantage
of it and become a tyrant. When Creon's son,

Haemon, tells him that popular opinion in Thebes is on Antigone's side, Creon answers (736) :

	Shall the city tell us, what orders I should give ?
Haemon.	These are the words of a rash youth.
Creon.	Should I rule this land for anyone else but myself ?
Haemon.	It is not a city if it belongs to a single man.
Creon.	Is not the city accounted the possession of the ruler ?
Haemon.	You would do well to be the monarch of a desert.

In so far as these lines and others in the same strain have a contemporary reference, Sophocles is reflecting the aristocratic fear of tyranny, which was not allayed by the theorising of Protagoras. Sophocles alludes twice to Protagoras' theories in the *Antigone*, on both occasions clearly asserting their danger,[1] and once uses Protagoras' word *euboulia* instead of the traditional " modesty " (*sophrosyne*) : Teiresias, perhaps to please Creon, says : " Does anyone know, or can anyone estimate how far the best of possessions is *euboulia* ? " It is therefore clear that Sophocles was at some pains to define his position in relation to Protagoras.

Alcaeus, Theognis, and the Eumenides of Aeschylus (if the interpretation quoted is right) at their different times voiced the complaints of the aristocrats against the prevailing regime. With the increase of democracy the conflict becomes sharper and the main problem of the *Antigone* is the clash between the individual, Antigone, and the state, represented by Creon. The play has predecessors in the *Prometheus Vinctus* of Aeschylus and the *Ajax* of Sophocles, both of which represent rebels against the state. The essential political differ-

[1] See *Greek Interpretations*, 51.

ence between them and the *Antigone* is that Prometheus, as far as we know, had no knowledge of what the effects of his theft of fire would be for him and we see only his punishment and not his original moment of decision, and Ajax, though a great personality and a rebel, acted in madness and committed suicide to avoid the consequences ; Antigone acts with her eyes open —she knows that Creon has decreed that Polynices' body is to be left unburied and that if anyone disobeys " his reward will be death by public stoning in the city " (35–6). She is quite alone ; her sister Ismene regards her proposal to bury Polynices as meddling in things that do not concern a woman : " You must remember that we were born women and cannot fight with men ; moreover we are ruled by those stronger than ourselves and must obey this and yet more painful orders " (61–4). The chorus of Theban elders (872) tell her that her " reverend action is a kind of reverence but the holder of power cannot allow his rules to be transgressed. You have been destroyed by your own self-willed spirit." She recognises herself in the end that her action is " in the city's despite " (907) but has no doubt of its rightness. She puts her position most clearly in her defence to Creon (450–70, tr. Bowra) :

It was not Zeus, I think, made this decree,
Nor Justice, dweller with the gods below
Who made appointment of such laws to men.
Nor did I think your edicts were so strong
That any mortal man should override
The gods' unwritten and undying laws.
Their life is not to-day or yesterday
But always, and none knoweth whence they came.
I could not pay the price before the gods
Of breaking these for fear of any man.

I knew that I should die ; and why not so ?
Though you had not ordained it.   If I die
Before my time, I count it something gained.
For whoso lives with many miseries
As I live, is not death a gain to him ?
Therefore I count the coming of this doom
No grief at all.   Rather, if I had left
Unburied mine own mother's son in death—
That would have grieved me.   This can bring no grief.
If what I do seems foolishness to you,
A foolish judgment reckons me a fool.

Antigone is an early martyr, or, in more modern terms,
the first conscientious objector, who appeals against the
particular enactments of the state to the ancestral
custom of honouring the dead.   This she claims is an
eternal law made by the gods, which she must obey
even at the cost of her life.

VI

THE realisation of the Periclean dream of democracy depended, as both Pericles and Protagoras saw, on respect for the law or rather for what the Greek called *nomos*, a much more comprehensive term than our Law. The Greek *nomos* includes the laws of the state, religious and ethical customs, local practices and institutions. Perhaps something like " the laws and traditions of the country " covers what Protagoras meant when he called *nomos* a great educative force. For the conservatives, like Sophocles in the *Antigone*, such *nomoi* were ultimately derived from the gods ; Protagoras tried to give them stability by finding Respect (*aidôs*) and Justice (*dike* or *dikaiosyne*) to be qualities existent in every human soul. At the moment, however, most advanced Greek thinkers were prepared to disregard *nomos* as manmade and inferior to *physis*, nature.

This is the culmination of a long development which started with the scientists in the Greek cities of Asia Minor. In the seventh century the Ionian commercial development had begun and these cities were in direct contact with the civilisations of the East. The scientists were primarily practical men : Thales (640–546 B.C.) foretold an eclipse, measured the pyramids by their shadow and imported a new technique of navigation from the Phoenicians ; Anaximander (610–546 B.C.) made the first Greek sundial and the first map of the world. But Ionian curiosity [1] coupled with the common Greek passion for simplification and systematisation demanded a more up-to-date

[1] Cf. *Greek Interpretations*, 25 f.

and credible account of the universe than that provided by earlier thinkers, Greek or foreign. It may have been that Oriental legends, which have found some echo in Homer and Hesiod,[1] first prompted Thales to look for the origin of the world in water, but his own experience of how ordinary physical things behave suggested that solids and gases could be derived from liquids and that earth floating on water was a more reasonable picture than the world tree of earlier cosmographers.[2] Anaximander altered the picture in two important ways : he explained the process of change by introducing the idea of retribution from the legal world : " Time arranges that things give satisfaction to one another for their injustices ", i.e. if sea encroaches on land in one place, sea has to give up land in another place. Secondly, he explained the heavenly bodies as pipes of air enclosing revolving fire on the analogy, as Professor Farrington has seen,[3] of the bellows of the blast furnace. Anaximenes (560–528 B.C.), the third of the early thinkers of Miletus, found in the felting industry an illustration for the change of the elements into one another.

The importance of this speculation, of which only the briefest and most summary account can be given here, was fourfold. First, the speculators were practical men living in the practical world and they explained the universe on the analogy of the practical world. Cosmogony ceased to be a preserve of priests and therefore of the aristocratic families who held priestly office, and further research to fill in the schematic picture was encouraged. Secondly, these speculators used the words God or The Divine to explain forces in the universe which could not be

---

[1] e.g. *Iliad*, xiv, 246.   [2] e.g. Hesiod, *Theogony*, 728.
[3] See for all this B. Farrington, *Character of early Greek Science*.

explained on the analogy of ordinary physical experience. They thus used the words God and Divine in an entirely new way and their God had nothing to do with the Olympians of Homer and Hesiod or with the gods of popular religion. Thirdly, where possible, they explained natural phenomena in mechanical terms and were moving towards the conception of laws of nature. A particular example will show the kind of effect that this view could have. The traditional view was that storms were due to the anger of Zeus at human injustice.[1] Anaximander, however, explained that all such phenomena were due to wind. This robbed Zeus of his weapons, and without this visible proof of his authority men might easily not only cease to believe in Zeus but also abandon the morality (*nomos*) which was believed to be supported by his authority.

In the fifth century the attack on *nomos* was carried further by the geographers and the doctors. Herodotus[2] tells the story of how certain Indians at Darius' court were horrified when they heard of the Greek custom of burning the dead and the Greeks were equally horrified at the Indians' custom of eating the bodies of their ancestors. When religious customs (*nomos*) of such sanctity as the treatment of the dead were shown to vary so flagrantly from place to place, it was difficult to believe wholeheartedly in the permanence and divinity of *nomos*. The doctors by accurate observation of diseases decided that all diseases could be attributed to natural causes and there was no justification for believing that certain diseases were visitations of the gods on the wicked, thus undermining still further divine authority and *nomos* in the sense of religious beliefs. Yet another weakening of *nomos* was clear to

[1] e.g. Homer, *Iliad*, xvi. 385, and above, p. 12.   [2] III, 38, 3.

see in the procedure of the democratic assembly ; what validity had *nomos* when it could be changed from day to day by a public meeting ? Thus grew up the antithesis between *nomos*, man-made and artificial, and *physis*, the real world of animal nature and human passions, in which the law of mechanical causation held, and with the antithesis the command to live according to *physis*.

The clearest statement of the principle and its consequences is in a fragment of the sophist Antiphon,[1] which has been dated 440–430 B.C. (B, 44A, 1) :

It is justice not to transgress the laws of the city in which a man lives. A man would most use justice to his own advantage if he were to regard the laws [*nomoi*] when in the presence of witnesses and the commands of nature [*physis*] when he is alone. The commands of law are artificial, those of nature necessary. The commands of law are the results of agreement ; the commands of nature are the result of growth, not of agreement. Therefore the transgressor of the law, if he escapes the notice of those who made the agreement, is free of dishonour and punishment, but not if he is seen. But suppose a man goes against possibility and does violence to something which has grown up in nature, if he escapes the notice of all men the harm is no less ; if all see him the harm is no greater. For the damage is not a matter of opinion but of reality. The point of this inquiry is that the majority of the rights laid down by law are at enmity with nature.

Critias, who was Plato's uncle and one of the leading politicians of the later fifth century, pushed the theory a stage further when he made a character in a play suggest that some cunning man had invented the gods to frighten men from committing the crimes which the law could not see (B, 25) :

[1] See Aly, *Formprobleme*, 104 ff.

There was a time when the life of men was disorderly and beastlike and the servant of strength, when the good had no prize and the bad no chastisement. Then, it seems to me, men imposed laws as chastisers, that justice [*dike*] might be a tyrant with *hybris* as its slave ; and anyone who transgressed was punished. Then, when the laws hindered them from open acts of violence but they continued where they could not be seen, then, it seems to me, a cunning and clever man invented the fear of the gods, that the wicked might be afraid even if their words and deeds and thoughts were unknown to the authorities. Therefore then he first introduced the divine, that god has eternal life and strength, hearing and sight, wisdom and attention, wearing a divine nature, who hears all that men say, sees all that men do, and if you silently plot a wrong, the gods will know it.

If you accept the antithesis between man-made *nomos* and the reality of *physis*, the consequences for moral and political theory depend on your interpretation of both terms, but particularly of *physis*. One interpretation is that in the world of nature (*physis*) the stronger fulfils all his desires at the expense of the weaker, and therefore the command to live according to nature means follow the dictates of passion and if you are caught use all the modern technique of rhetoric to avoid the punishment which you deserve. This is neatly put by the Unjust Argument (a personification of the power of rhetoric) in Aristophanes' *Clouds*, 1075 :

I will speak next of the necessities of nature [*physis*]. You sinned, you fell in love, you committed adultery, and then you were caught. You are lost for you have no eloquence. But let me be your friend and you can enjoy nature, sport and laugh, think nothing dishonourable. For if you are caught in adultery, you will answer that you have committed no crime. You can put the responsibility on Zeus ; he was the slave of love and women. How can you, a mortal, be stronger than a god ?

Transferred to the political sphere the analogy of the animal world justifies the position taken up by the Athenians when they annexed the little island of Melos in 416 B.C. (Thuc. V, 85 f.) : [1] they are strong enough not to fear hurt and therefore they can exact what they please. They have no need of convention but can live under the law of nature according to which men rule whatever they conquer. In internal politics it justifies the argument of the sophist Thrasymachus, recorded by Plato in the first book of the *Republic*, that the government is always the stronger and pursues its own desires, imposing them as laws (*nomoi*) on the subjects. An eloquent exposition of the same political doctrine is given by Callicles in Plato's *Gorgias* ; he ends (483c) :

For on what principle of justice did Xerxes invade Hellas or his father the Scythians ? (not to speak of numberless other examples). These men act according to nature ; not perhaps according to the law which we impose. We try to mould the best and strongest of our children, taking them young like lion cubs ; we try to make them our slaves by incantations and spells, saying that equality is right and that honour and justice consist in equality. But supposing a man had sufficient natural force, he will shake all this off and break through it and escape, he will trample under foot our formulas and spells and charms and laws which are all contrary to nature ; our slave rebels and is revealed as our master, and then natural justice shines forth.

It is an old maxim of Greek poetry that however charming lion cubs may be in their extreme youth, in

[1] *Greek Interpretations*, 69.

the end they run amok ; Helen is compared to one by Aeschylus (*Ag.* 620 f.). Herodotus (VI, 131) says that Pericles' mother dreamt that she was giving birth to a lion a few days before she bore him. Aristophanes (*Frogs*, 1432–3) compares Alcibiades to a lion's cub. Natural justice is, of course, the principle that the strong rule whatever they can control. This is the philosophical background of the power politics and revolutions of the last quarter of the fifth century B.C.

It is easy to condemn the sophists, as Plato and his successors condemned them, and it is true that they provided the intellectual tools for the unscrupulous like Alcibiades and Critias. The problem is of some interest to us because the sophists represent also the emancipation of thought by science from magic and religion. The dangers of this position are obvious both in political life and in private life where those who regarded themselves as emancipated from the traditional religion also thought that they were free of morality.

Other interpretations of *physis* are possible. The conditions of life in fifth-century Athens, where foreigners and resident aliens (*metoikoi*) worked side by side with Athenian citizens, and on some public works, probably also in the potteries, slaves and freemen received the same wages for the same tasks, gave birth to the conception of the brotherhood of man. Antiphon (B, 44B) phrased this : " in nature all men are alike, both barbarians and Greeks ". Hippias of Elis in Plato's *Protagoras* (337c) regards all wise men of any Greek city as " kinsmen and friends and fellow-citizens by nature but not by law. For like is akin to like by nature, but law, being tyrant over men, does violence to many things contrary to nature." This line of thought probably did not have many adherents in the nationalist world of the late fifth century, but it laid the foundations of later cosmopolitanism, and prepared for an entirely new view of slavery. The old man in Euripides' *Ion* (854) says : " One thing makes slaves ashamed, their name. In everything else a slave is no worse than a freeman, if he is good." The conservative writer of the time of the Peloponnesian War, whose work is preserved under the title of Xenophon, *Constitution of the Athenians*, known to modern scholars as the Old Oligarch, gives a pleasing picture (i, 10) :

Slaves and foreigners have the greatest licence in Athens ; you may not beat a slave there nor will a slave get out of your way. If it were customary for freemen to beat slave or foreigner or freedman, they would often beat Athenians by mistake. For the common people do not wear better clothes than slaves or foreigners, nor are they better in appearance.

One of Plato's criticisms of the full Athenian democracy is that slaves are no less free than their owners (*Rep.* 563b).

Can we go a stage further and say that here we are on the brink of a new ideal of the citizen, the citizen who freely admits the existence of two worlds, a world of *nomos*, which is man-made and imperfect but at least prevents his doing or suffering major damage among his fellow-men, and a world of *physis*, the world of his lowest passions but also of his highest desires in thought, literature, and art ? Such a man will draw the conclusion : " If I am to be allowed freedom for the world of *physis*, I must conform to the world of *nomos*, and because *nomos* is man-made, I can at least see that *nomoi* are made that will give everybody the

greatest possible freedom to live in the world of *physis*."
Antiphon himself, from whom we started this discussion, is reported to have said that there is no greater
evil than anarchy (B, 61), and if it is true that he
devised the moderate oligarchy of 411 B.C., that may
have been his considered attempt to devise *nomoi*
which would leave the greatest possible freedom to
physis. The essence of this view of life is a kind of
double citizenship. The man must not only be by
law (*nomos*) a citizen of his own city but also by nature
(*physis*) citizen of a better world with eternal standards.
Antigone, according to Sophocles, chose death rather
than sacrifice the eternal laws of the gods and nature
to the transitory decrees of Creon. Socrates chose
the same path.

Socrates was born in 469 B.C. and must have been
well off, as he served in the heavy infantry during the
Peloponnesian War. He conceived it as his divine
mission (*Apology*, 23b) to search for wisdom, questioning
all who pretended to wisdom, craftsmen, statesmen, and
sophists, because he believed that if we knew what was
right we should do it. Plato puts this account of his
mission into his mouth in the *Apology* (29d) : he has
been offered acquittal on condition that he ceases
philosophising, and he answers :

I shall obey the god rather than you and, as long as I
breathe and am capable, I shall never cease philosophising
and encouraging you and pointing out to anyone I meet,
using my accustomed language : " You are an Athenian
and Athens is the greatest and most renowned city in
wisdom and strength : are you not ashamed that you care
for money, for making as much as possible, and for reputation and authority, but you do not have a care or a thought
for wisdom and truth and the improvement of your soul ? "
And if any one of you argues and says he cares, I shall not

let him go nor go away myself but I shall question him
and examine him and test him, and if he seems to me not
to possess virtue in fact but only in his own opinion, I shall
reproach him that he is putting the lowest value on that
which is of greatest value and greatest value on what is of
less value.   This I shall do to young and old, whomsoever
I meet, foreigner and Athenian, but particularly Athenians
because you are nearest me in birth.   For this is the order
of the god.

In this passage Socrates states both his aim and his
method.   His aim is to persuade his fellow-Athenians
to care for their souls instead of money or reputation or
official authority, the world of *nomos*.   The virtue of
the soul is more important than wealth or position,
and can be achieved by training (*askesis*), which includes training of the body to have minimum needs
(*autarkeia*) so that it will serve the soul (see
Xen. *Mem.* II, i), and which leads to moral self-control
(*enkrateia*) " the foundation of virtue " (Xen.
Mem. II, v, 4) ; the man who is master of himself
is truly free (Xen. *Mem.* I, v, 5–6).   Socrates regards
himself as an educator promoting the health of the
soul, just as the doctor promotes the health of the body
(Plato, *Laches*, 185e ; cf. Jaeger, *Paideia*, II, 38).
The treatment is scientific, as Greek doctoring had
become, and consists of ceaseless question and answer
until the underlying general idea behind the particular
manifestations of it is discovered ; when it has been
discovered, it becomes a source of action in the soul
and the soul is better for it.   Thus according to Plato
(*Protagoras*, 345d) Socrates criticises Simonides' praise
of the man " whoever of his own free will does nothing
ugly " : [1]   Socrates says that no man of his own free
will does wrong ; he implies that the man who does

[1] Cf. above, p. 23, and Jaeger, *Paideia*, II, 68.

wrong does not do it from will, which is informed by
knowledge, but from desire, which is not. He has
pushed beyond the Simonidean conception to the
deeper conception of a trained will informed by
knowledge of what is right.

We can see the tradition behind Socrates' view of
life : *askesis* was practised by the great trainers of
competitors for the Panhellenic games such as Melesias,
the father of Socrates' older friend Thucydides, and
enkrateia is not essentially different from the old virtue
of *sophrosyne* (modesty), preached by Pindar and
Sophocles and the sculptures of the Parthenon.
Simonides' ideal of purity of motive is a precursor of
Socrates' ethics, so is Theognis' praise of justice as the
epitome of virtue ; we may guess that Sophocles'
Antigone was an inspiration to him when he saw it at
the age of twenty-six. His technique of argument he
borrowed from the sophists, and this is the truth
behind the caricature of Socrates as a sophist in
Aristophanes' *Clouds*. The cause of Socrates' unpar-
alleled influence on later Greek thought is twofold,
his ideal of the " health of the soul " (with a suggestion
of the means for pursuing it) and his life spent in
realising this ideal.

Socrates took no unnecessary part in state business.
Apragmosyne (quietness) was one of the characteristics
of the Athenian aristocrats, and Pericles branded such
men as useless ; Plato has recorded Socrates' own
defence (*Apology*, 32c) :

perhaps it would seem absurd that I take so much trouble
in giving you all this private advice when I have never had
the courage to stand up before the demos and give public
advice on affairs of state. The reason is something you
have often heard me tell you, that I have a divine voice,
which Meletus ridicules in the indictment. I have had

it from childhood, and whenever it comes it always warns
me off something I am going to do, but never tells me to
do anything. This is what prevents me from public business and I think that has been a very good thing. For you
must understand that if I had long ago tried to enter
politics I should long ago have perished and have helped
neither you nor myself. For no man is likely to remain
safe who opposes either you or any other popular assembly,
and tries to prevent the many illegal and unjust acts that
are done in politics ; he who will fight for the right, if
he would live even for a short time, must have a private
station and not a public one. I will give you good evidence
of this, not words but deeds, which you prefer. . . . I
never held public office but I was a member of the Boule,
and my tribe Antiochis was in office when you decided
to condemn the whole body of ten generals who failed to
pick up the dead after the sea battle, which was contrary
to the law as you later decided. Then I alone of the
presidents opposed your acting illegally and voted against
you. The orators were ready to impeach and arrest me,
and you shouted approval, but I thought I ought rather
to run the risk with law and justice on my side than to
side with you in your unjust designs through fear of death
and imprisonment.

This is the spirit of Antigone, of individualist idealism
which is ready to die for a higher standard.

Socrates distinguishes very clearly between the law
itself and the particular misapplication of it. He
makes the same distinction in Plato's *Crito* : during
the period when he was in prison, between the passing
of the death sentence and its execution, his friends had
made arrangements to smuggle him out of prison and
over the border to safety. Socrates refused to go ;
he imagined that the Laws and the Community came
and asked him (50a) :

What is it you are thinking of doing ? Do you mean

by this action to destroy the laws and the whole city ?   Do you think a city can exist in any stability if sentences passed have no validity but are upset by private individuals ? . . . We brought you into the world and nurtured and educated you and gave you and every other citizen a share in every good which we had to give, we further proclaim to any citizen by the liberty which we allow him, that if he does not like us when he has become of age and has seen the ways of the city and has made our acquaintance, he may take his goods and go anywhere else he pleases. . . . Now you depart in innocence, a sufferer and not a doer of evil, the victim not of us laws but of men. But if you escape and thereby answer their injustice with injustice, transgressing your agreement and covenant with us and injuring yourself and your friends and your country and us, we shall be angry with you while you live and in the grave our brothers the laws in Hades will not receive you kindly, knowing that you tried to destroy us too as far as you could.

There is a world of difference between Socrates' individualism within the state and the stateless individualism of a younger contemporary, Aristippus of Cyrene, who, as Jaeger [1] says, saw

the inevitable conflict between the spiritually free individual and the community with its inevitable tyranny . . . [Men of his type] lived in foreign countries as resident aliens, so as to be free of all civic duties, and built themselves an ivory tower on this unsteady foundation.

We have noticed already the likeness between Socrates and Sophocles' Antigone ; the essential mark of this type of citizen is that he does his duty as a citizen because his true loyalty is to something else, which may very likely be religion. I think a case can be made both from his life and from his plays that Euripides had the same ideal ; that he believed in the

[1] *Paideia*, II, 72.

Athenian democracy is clear from his patriotic plays, particularly his defence of equality of law and equality of opportunity in the *Suppliants* (229 f., 403 f.) and of equality in the *Phoenissae* (531) [1] ; it is also clear that he hated the unscrupulous politician and the time-serving official (*Andr.* 694 ff. ; *Suppl.* 229 f., 412 f. ; *Phoen.* 531 f.). His sympathy was with Hippolytus, who wanted to be first in Hellenic games but second in the city with the best of friends (1016), with Ion, who prized " leisure, the dearest thing a man can have," more highly than political life at Athens (634), with Amphion, the young musician of the *Antiope* (fr. 194), who regarded the quiet man as a safe friend to friends and best in the city, and with the farmer who spoke against the mob in the popular assembly at Argos (*Orestes*, 917 ff., tr. Meredith) :

> No beauty, he, but a man that was a man
> Not greatly exercised in city contacts,
> A working farmer, backbone of the state ;
> Good enough at debating when he wished ;
> Sound and a man whose record was unstained.

All these, like the historical Socrates, had their true interests not in the momentary successes of political debate, but in something outside the political world, such as religion, art, athletics, or the country. These things are outside the world of *nomos*, laws and conventions and money, with its artificial and transitory standards. They have a perfection which belongs in some sense to the fabric of the world, to *physis*, and those whose standards are formed by these eternal values have a sober and disinterested judgment in the everyday world of *nomos*.

[1] Professor Morrison has discussed the relation of these passages to Protagoras in *Classical Quarterly*, XXXV.

VII

ARISTOPHANES AND THUCYDIDES

ARISTOPHANES and Thucydides in their different ways provide the most enlightening commentary on Athens during the Peloponnesian War, which covered most of the last third of the fifth century B.C. Aristophanes produced his comedies in Athens at two annual festivals of Dionysus from 427 B.C. until well into the fourth century B.C. Although, as Professor Gomme [1] has recently pointed out, Aristophanes was primarily a dramatist and therefore considers everything primarily from the point of view of comic effect, nevertheless he was an extremely acute observer, and his plays are at least as valuable a commentary to us now as a file of Low's cartoons will be to historians in the future. Thucydides the historian was a younger relation of Thucydides son of Melesias, who opposed Pericles, but, as Professor Wade-Gery [2] says, " the younger Thucydides was caught wholly by the glamour of Pericles ; he thinks his principate (gained over the elder Thucydides' body) most admirable . . . Pericles made him drunk with the idea of power, nor to the end of his life did Thucydides forget it."

Thucydides saw the " true cause " of the Peloponnesian War, which was, however, " the least mentioned " in the growth of Athens, fear of which compelled the Spartans to make war. More definitely, the Athenian western policy, noticed above [3] and culminating in the alliance with Corcyra in 433 B.C., threatened the food trade from the West to the Pelo-

---

[1] *Classical Review*, LII, 97.
[2] *Journal of Hellenic Studies*, 1932, 221.　　[3] See p. 42.

ponnese ; a single but very obvious symptom of Athenian western expansion can be seen in the fact that Athenian pottery drove out all competitors in the Western market. Thucydides is probably right in seeing the true cause of war in Spartan fear of Athenian power rather than in the opposition of their two ideologies, which had in fact co-existed for a very long time. The first ten years of war ended in something like stalemate because Sparta had all the power on land and Athens all the power by sea. Athens could not be reduced by an annual invasion at harvest time because the Athenians could shut themselves up within their fortifications and live on foreign corn.

Three events in the earlier years of the war gave Thucydides occasion for especially penetrating reflection on the forces at work : the death of Pericles in 429 B.C., the revolution in Corcyra and the revolt of Mitylene in 427 B.C. Pericles himself died of the plague ; Thucydides' eulogy of Pericles has already been quoted.[1] At the same time he discusses the causes of Athenian defeat. Pericles' successors abandoned his advice and

both their direct military policy and their other policy was governed by their private ambitions [the aristocrats] and their private interests [the democrats], which was bad both for Athens and her allies because their success brought honour and profit to individuals and their failure damaged the war effort of the whole city. [Then follows the characterisation of Pericles.] His successors were more on an equality with one another and, each desiring to be supreme, they were ready to surrender the whole conduct of affairs to the whims of the people ;

thus Thucydides ascribes both the failure of the Sicilian expedition in 415 B.C. and the final defeat of

[1] See p. 47.

Athens to the selfish intrigues of the various politicians. Protagoras had said that oligarchy leads to rivalries between leading men resulting in civil war and democracy leads to parties within the state, who combine to rob the state for their private gain ; writing some forty years later Thucydides applies Protagoras' justification of the Periclean protocracy to Athenian history after Pericles, and finds that on the whole it fits because Pericles' successors lacked his combination of genius and incorruptibility.

The revolution in Corcyra in 427 B.C., which ended in a mass murder of the aristocratic party by the democratic party, inspired Thucydides to analyse the phenomena of revolution (III, 82). Revolutions in the various Greek states had, according to him, two causes, first that it was possible in time of war to invoke foreign aid, and second that wartime restrictions sharpen tempers (82/2).

The tie of political clubs was stronger than the tie of family because unquestioning daring [the word used for acts of *hybris*] was found more readily in the former ; for political clubs do not seek the public good in accordance with the law but private interest in defiance of the law, and their internal loyalty is not based on divine law [like the association of the *polis* which depends on *Dike* the daughter of Zeus] but on partnership in transgressing the law [82/6]. . . . [82/8] The cause of all this was the basing of conduct in office on private interest [democrats] and private ambition [aristocrats], and from these two motives came the passion which they displayed in the contest. The leaders in the cities used idealistic vocabulary, paying lip-service on the democratic side to political equality [*isonomia*] and on the aristocratic side to modesty [*sophrosyne*], while they made the public interests, to which they were devoted in name, in reality their prize.

A picture of post-Periclean Athens is given in Thucydides' account of the revolt of Mitylene in 427 B.C. When the town had been captured, the Athenian assembly decided to put to death all the Mitylenaeans of military age and enslave the women and children. " The next day they felt a kind of repentance and reflected that a decision to destroy a whole city and not only the guilty was savage and arrogant " (III, 36/4). The friends of the Mitylenaeans in Athens persuaded the authorities to bring the matter before the assembly again. Thucydides has reported the speech made to the assembly by Cleon " who had carried the earlier resolution to put the Mitylenaeans to death ; he was the most violent of the Athenians and had a long way the greatest power of persuasion with the people at that time " (III, 36/6). Cleon was a tanner and, according to Aristotle (*Athp.* 28/3), " he was the first to shout and use abusive language from the platform and made his public speeches in his shirt-sleeves at a time when it was customary to wear frock coats ". Cleon's arguments for not reversing the previous decree are interesting : " You do not realise that your empire is a tyranny exercised over unwilling subjects who are always conspiring against you. . . . Your rule depends on your strength and not on their goodwill " (III, 37/2). This is realistic recognition of the change in character of the Athenian empire, which was implicitly accepted forty years before when the Persian War ended and the attempts of the first allies to break away were suppressed ; here the naked truth is stated, as clearly as in the Melian Dialogue. Cleon goes on to say (III, 37/3) that it is intolerable if resolutions of the people cannot stand and if it is not realised that a city is stronger with inferior but unalterable laws (*nomoi*) than with good laws which are not allowed to stand ; stupidity coupled with modesty is more profitable than cleverness coupled with lack of morals ; the simpler sort generally run the city better than the more astute.

The more astute want to appear cleverer than the laws [*nomoi*] and to win in debates on state affairs, as being the greatest arena for their talents, and thereby often ruin their cities. The others, mistrusting their own intelligence, admit that the laws are wiser than themselves and being incapable of criticising a clever speaker are impartial judges rather than participants, and so for the most part judge right.

We need not follow the rest of the debate ; Cleon's antagonist won the day by pleading the expediency of mercy for keeping the rest of the empire in subjection, and a ship was sent to Mitylene with all speed to prevent the execution being put into effect.

There are several points of interest in Cleon's speech, although much of it is obviously special pleading and Cleon is catching votes by treating the assembly's decree of the day before as an " ancestral law ". The first is the statement that the ordinary man keeps the city straight because the amateur judgment is better than the arguments of the rhetorician. It is in line with Protagoras' theory [1] that every citizen should be expected to possess the political virtues of Justice and Respect, which is the reason for admitting a smith's or a cobbler's counsel in public affairs. A further development of the idea is found in the speech of the Syracusan democratic statesman Hermocrates (Thuc. VI, 39) :

It will be said that democracy is neither intelligent nor fair [*ison*]. . . . But I say first that the people is the name

[1] See above, p. 51.

of the whole and oligarchy the name of a part [*meros*], secondly that the rich are the best guardians of money, the intelligent would give the best advice, and the many would give the best judgment when they had heard, and in democracy these elements both for themselves and as a whole have equal privileges [*isomoirein*].

This is the theory of a balanced democracy in which experts perform according to their expertise but the final decision rests on the amateur judgment of common sense.

Secondly, Cleon stresses the susceptibility of the Athenian assembly to rhetoric and its readiness to give its votes for beauty of language rather than soundness of subject-matter and argument. Although in Cleon's mouth this merely means " listen to my speeches but don't listen to the idealism of the intellectuals ", it must be remembered that Protagoras claimed to be able to teach his pupils to be potent speakers in public business, and other sophists offered to teach men to make the worse appear the better reason. The dangers of this kind of sophistic teaching is the theme of Aristophanes' *Clouds*, where there is a debate between the Just and the Unjust Argument,[1] and in the *Acharnians*, produced in 425 B.C., Aristophanes claims that his satire has done something to discredit the rhetoricians :

Let honour and praise be the guerdon, he says, of the poet whose satire has stayed you
From believing the orators' novel conceits wherewith they cajoled and betrayed you ;
Who bids you despise adulation and lies nor be citizens Vacant and Vain.
For before, when an embassy came from the states intriguing your favour to gain,

[1] See above, p. 60.

And called you the town of the violet crown, so grand and
    exalted you grew
That at once on your tiptails erect you would sit, those
    Crowns were so pleasant to you.
And then if they added the shiny, they got whatever they
    asked for their praises.
Though apter, I ween, for an oily sardine than for you and
    your city the phrase is.

                            (*Ach.* 133 f., tr. Rogers)

Aristophanes' play of the next year, February 424 B.C.,
was a direct attack on Cleon after one of his most
successful military exploits, the capture of the Spartan
force on Sphacteria. In the *Knights*, a sausage-seller
is put up to overcome Cleon and when the sausage-
seller doubts his ability to be " steward of the people "
(the word used of the Periclean monarch in Hdt. III, 82)
he is answered (213, tr. Murray) :

> Easy as lying ! do as you now do,
> Turn every question to a public stew,
> Hash things and cook things. Win the common herd
> By strong sweet sauces in your every word.
> For other gifts you have half the catalogue
> Already, for the perfect demagogue :
> A bloodshot voice, low breeding, huckster's tricks—
> What more can man require for politics ?

When Cleon has been defeated, the sausage-seller
rejuvenates the elderly Demos so that he appears once
more " as he was when he sat at Miltiades' side and
with great Aristides at mess ", in the first days of the
Persian Wars. " No longer he smells of balloting
shells but of myrrh and of peace running down "
(1334, tr. Murray). In spite of Aristophanes' plea for
peace in this play and the *Acharnians*, Athens rejected
the Spartan offer of peace after Sphacteria. It is

hard to avoid the conclusion that the Athenians, though theoretically possessed of "modesty and justice", were not at this time practically capable of withstanding the new art of public rhetoric, whether used by the conservative or the democratic politician.

The third point, which is common to all the three passages of Thucydides quoted above and to the Melian Dialogue, is Thucydides' assumption that not only foreign policy but also the political conduct of the Athenian at home was entirely governed by selfish motives, that, as Thucydides says in his account of Revolution, conduct in office was based on private interest and private ambitions. The ethics of grab, if this interpretation of the *physis–nomos* antithesis given in the last chapter may be so described, are accepted by Thucydides as the explanation of Athenian politics in the Peloponnesian War and recognised, though deplored, by Aristophanes.

Peace was made with Sparta in 421 B.C., but did not last. In 415 B.C. the Athenians sent their expedition to Sicily. Success should have meant complete victory, because if the Greeks in Italy and Sicily joined the Athenian confederacy, the whole of the western trade would be in Athenian hands : the plan was made by the young and brilliant Alcibiades, a near relation of Pericles but a product of the modern sophistic education with no standard except self-interest. When the expedition had started, Alcibiades' opponents brought a suit against him and got him condemned in absence ; Alcibiades fled to Sparta and persuaded the Spartans to send a Spartan general to Sicily and to fortify a strong point in Attic territory. The conservative Athenian Strategos Nicias made mistake after mistake, but was not finally defeated until 413 B.C. ; even then the Athenians lasted the best part of ten years and, as Thucydides says, they did not give in until they were brought down by their internal disagreements.

The history of this last period does not concern us except in so far as it embraced constitutional changes. In 412 B.C. Alcibiades fled from Sparta and started intriguing with the Persian Tissaphernes ; he then suggested to the Athenians at Samos that if they would abolish the democracy he could bring the great king over to their side. Peisander brought these proposals to Athens, and after a long debate in the assembly won the day by pointing out that Persian help against Sparta could only be bought at the price of " more orderly politics and magistracies confined to the few " (Thuc. VIII, 53/3). Peisander was sent back to negotiate with Tissaphernes but the negotiations failed. Nevertheless, by 411 B.C., when Peisander returned to Athens, the oligarchical clubs had already made full preparations, and the assembly empowered a board of commissioners to frame a constitution (Thuc. VIII, 67). The brains behind this was Antiphon, who is thus characterised by Thucydides (VIII, 68) :

inferior in virtue [*arete*] to none of his contemporaries and most gifted both in thought and in expression . . . he was suspected by the people because of his reputation for cleverness [compare Cleon's speech in the Mitylenaean debate for the democrats' fear of intellect]. . . . Another leader of the revolutionary party was Theramenes, the son of Hagnon, a good speaker and a good planner. No wonder then that in the hands of all these able men the attempt, however arduous, succeeded. For it certainly was not an easy thing, one hundred years after the fall of the tyrants, to destroy the liberties of the Athenians.

The actual constitution passed is extremely obscure in detail, but its main outlines seem to be as follows.

For the immediate emergency, the power was to be in the hands of a Council of 400. The permanent constitution was to be based on an assembly of 5,000 over thirty years of age ; this probably amounted to about one-fifth of the number who had previously been eligible to attend the assembly. The 5,000 were to be divided into quarters, and a committee of each quarter was to form the Council and to elect the Strategoi and the nine archons and the treasury officials for the year from its own quarter of the 5,000. The original 400 lasted four months, during which time they made an unsuccessful peace offer to the Spartans and lost Euboea. Theramenes was largely responsible for the transference of power to the 5,000 ; according to Thucydides (VIII, 97/2), this was the best government in his day : for it contained a moderate blend of oligarchy and democracy. The restriction of the assembly was a throwback to the time before Solon, and the new constitution could only be called a blend of oligarchy and democracy by contrast with the much more restricted oligarchy of the Thirty.

With the return of Alcibiades the full democracy was restored. The war dragged on with varying success until the decisive defeat of the Athenian fleet at Aegospotami in 404 B.C. The Athenians were then forced to accept Spartan terms. The Spartan general Lysander imposed an oligarchy of Thirty, headed by the aristocrat Critias, Plato's uncle, whose advanced theories about the gods we have already had occasion to quote. The government was based on 1,000 men, presumably the first property class only, from whom the Council of 500 and the other magistrates were chosen. Once their power was established, they proceeded to use it to plunder the wealthy and put 1,500 men to death. After a civil war of great ferocity

Thrasybulus restored the democracy in 403 B.C. and the Spartans had to accept the restoration.

Critias and his friends had tried to realise in Athens the sophistic theory that justice is the expediency of the stronger. No more eloquent testimony to their perversion of government can be found than Plato, who was no lover of democracy (*Ep.* VII, 324d) :

Some of them were friends and relations of mine, and they immediately invited me to take part as the business would suit me. I was young and I thought that their government would lead the city from the unjust life to a life of justice ; therefore I watched them carefully to see what they would achieve. And seeing that in a short time they made the former government appear golden by contrast . . . I was distressed and dissociated myself from their cruelty.

As an example of their methods, the case of Theramenes, the moderate who had secured the transfer of power to the 5,000 in 411 B.C. and did much to negotiate the peace with Sparta and now persuaded Critias to broaden the basis of government by choosing a list of 3,000, has become famous. According to the new constitution members of the 3,000 could only be tried by the Council ; everybody else could be put to death without trial by the Thirty. Theramenes was a member of the 3,000, but when the Council showed every sign of acquitting him, Critias called in his soldiers, struck him off the list of the 3,000, and had him put to death.

Among those murdered by the Thirty was Polemarchus, the brother of the orator Lysias. Their father was Cephalus of Syracuse, who had been persuaded by Pericles to set up a shield-factory in Athens and had been an extremely successful business man, a resident alien (*metoikos*) of the kind that had been

encouraged since Solon's time ; his house is the setting
for Plato's *Republic*. Lysias afterwards prosecuted
Eratosthenes, one of the Thirty, for the murder of his
brother, and his description of the scene is worth
quoting (*Or.* XII, 17) :

To Polemarchus the Thirty gave their customary command, to drink hemlock, before saying for what reason he
was to be put to death. So little had he of trial and
defence. And when he was carried from the prison dead,
though we had three houses they did not allow the funeral
to take place from any one of them, but hired a hut and laid
the body there. And though we had many garments they
did not give us one, when we asked, for the burial, but his
friends gave one a garment, one a pillow, and others
whatever they had for his burial. And though they had
seven hundred shields of ours, though they had silver and
gold, bronze and ornaments and furniture and women's
garments more than they had ever thought they would
possess, and a hundred and twenty slaves of whom they
took the best and gave the others to the treasury, they went
to these lengths of greed and avidity and gave an exhibition
of their own character. The golden earrings of Polemarchus' wife which she was wearing when first he came
into the house, Melobius took out of her ears. And we
were not pitied by them in the smallest part of our wealth.
But they were more savage because of our money than
others would have been when angered by great crimes,
though we had not deserved this in Athens but had performed all liturgies, paid many taxes, shown ourselves
orderly and obedient, though we had no enemy but had
ransomed many Athenians from their foes. So they treated
us foreigners, who had behaved very differently from them
who were citizens. For they drove many citizens into the
arms of the enemy, killed many unjustly and left them
without burial, disfranchised many who were enfranchised,
prevented many from marrying off their daughters. And
they are so bold that they come here to make their defence

and say that they have done nothing base or shameful. I could wish they spoke true for I should have no small share in this blessing. But now they cannot plead this either to the city or to me. For my brother, as I said before, was killed by Eratosthenes, not because he had suffered any private injury from him nor because he had seen him committing any public offence, but because Eratosthenes was the ready slave of his own lawlessness.

The trial of Eratosthenes was one of the political prosecutions which inevitably followed the restoration of the democracy. Another was the trial of Socrates, who had been the friend of Thucydides, son of Melesias, and was regarded as the teacher of Critias ; he was condemned and put to death in 399 B.C.

The speeches written for aristocratic defendants in lawsuits during these years show the sort of arguments that might win a democratic jury's respect and outweigh even a suspicion of having acted with the oligarchy in 411 or 403 B.C. Evidence is produced for loyalty to the constitution and the city, for public services as a real contribution to the city's wealth, and the " orderly " and " modest " private life of those " who mind their own business ". The fact that these conservative catchwords can still be used without prejudicing the defendants is some evidence of the reality of the amnesty between political parties.

The law-court speeches also emphasise the power of the professional speakers, a theme mentioned earlier in connection with Cleon. According to Lysias some politicians are more interested in what they can make for themselves than in the good of the state. If state officials commit crimes they can pay speech-writers to get them off in the law-courts by threatening the jury with losing their pay. As a result the politicians live in great houses while the people of Athens have become their slaves instead of their masters.

Through all these charges and counter-charges, two ideas come out clearly as the foundations of the new democracy. Speech after speech refers to *homonoia*—the unanimity of all classes in the restoration ; the amnesty which resulted in this *homonoia* is held up as a unique example of a peaceful end to a revolution, which gave Athens the reputation of wisdom and modesty. In one of his few law-court speeches Isocrates enlarges on the theme (XVIII, 27) : *homonoia* depends on the covenant of the amnesty—covenants are the bases of human civilisation and the foundation of private business as well as national and international dealings. The second idea is the old Periclean idea of *nomos* as the laws and traditions of Athens ; the new democracy is seen as the rule of law and the revolutions of 411 and 403 B.C. are described as " scorn of the law ". These two ideas were the basis of Pericles' dream and Protagoras' theory and are the leading ideas also of the fourth century.

VIII

PLATO

PLATO was born in 427 B.C. His father was an aristocrat, Ariston; his mother was descended from a kinsman of Solon; his uncle was Critias, the leader of the Thirty Tyrants. A letter written to the Sicilians about 353 B.C. contains so much autobiography that much is worth quoting. After describing his disillusionment with the government of the Thirty, he goes on (*Ep.* VII, 325a) :

And in a short time the Thirty and its government fell and again, though slowly, the desire for a political life tugged at me. It was a time of disturbance and naturally many distressing things occurred, and it was not surprising that personal vengeances were exacted on a greater scale than in quiet times, although on the whole returning exiles behaved extremely well. Nevertheless fortune willed that my friend Socrates should be brought to law by some of the more powerful politicians on a charge which was most unjust and least befitted Socrates, for he was charged, condemned and put to death for impiety. . . . This made me reflect; and the more I considered the character of politicians and contemporary laws and customs and the older I got, the more difficult I felt an honest political career to be for myself. For it was not possible to act without friends and loyal companions, who were not easy to find now; for Athens was not running on the same lines now as in our fathers' time [he is probably thinking both of the organisation of the aristocratic opposition to Pericles by Thucydides, son of Melesias (above, p. 46), and of the oligarchical clubs which brought about the revolution in 411 B.C. (above, p. 78)] and it was impossible to get new friends without excessive difficulty. Laws and customs were being corrupted at such a rate that, although

I had been at first full of zeal for politics, when I observed this and saw everything in a state of flux, I was in the end completely dizzy. I did not cease thinking how improvements could be made both in the government of Athens and in the theory of government, but I waited for the right occasion for action, and in the end I perceived that all cities in Greece now are badly governed, for the state of the laws can hardly be cured without a combination of fortune and miraculous energy, and I was compelled to say in praise of true philosophy that only philosophy gives a complete view of justice as it concerns both the city and the individual. Therefore the human race will not be delivered from evil until either those who are genuine philosophers achieve political power or the rulers in the cities are led by some divine grace to philosophise. With these thoughts in my mind I came to Italy and Sicily the first time [388/7 B.C.].

He then tells how he was shocked by the excesses of luxury there and inferred that these cities would suffer continual revolutions and be governed by tyrants, oligarchs, and democrats in turn, and that their rulers would not even endure the sound of (326d) " a just constitution with equality of law " ; the picture clearly is of great inequalities of wealth, giving rise to frequent changes of government. Plato then describes what happened in Syracuse, where he met the young Dion. He was the son-in-law of Dionysius the Elder, the tyrant of Syracuse, who had defended Syracuse against a Carthaginian attack in 405 B.C. and had then succeeded in uniting Sicily and much of South Italy under his rule (327a).

I did not realise that by telling him my ideals for men and advising him to practise them I was in fact contriving the breakdown of the tyranny. For Dion who was extremely receptive especially of what I told him then, was the keenest and most attentive listener of all the young men that I have ever met and was willing to live for the rest of his life differently from the majority of Greeks in Italy and Sicily, having accepted virtue as more valuable than pleasure or luxury.

When Dionysius the Elder died in 367 B.C., Dion (327c)

thought that it was in every way necessary that I should come to Syracuse as quickly as possible to co-operate with him, remembering how easily his association with me had brought him to desire the life which is best and most honourable. If he could achieve the same in Dionysius [the son and successor of the tyrant] as he intended, he had great hopes of avoiding slaughter and death and all the evils that have actually come to pass [Plato is writing this fourteen years later after Dion had been banished by the younger Dionysius, had returned and driven the younger Dionysius out again and had finally himself been murdered] and of establishing a life of happiness and truth in the whole country.

Although Plato hesitated greatly, in particular doubted the possibility of educating the younger Dionysius, he decided to go, partly out of loyalty to his former pupil Dion, partly because it was the kind of " right occasion for action " for which Plato had been waiting and he was ashamed to be (328c) " pure theory and never willing to tackle practice ". (329b) " So conforming to reason and justice, as far as humanly possible, and abandoning my own activities, which had by then a considerable reputation, I went to live under a tyranny which seemed compatible neither with my doctrines nor with me."

The subsequent history of Plato's Sicilian experiment will occupy us briefly later. We must now examine what led up to it. Plato tells us that his natural desire, as a young aristocrat, to take part in politics was killed first by the excesses of the Thirty Tyrants in 404 B.C., then by the excesses of the restored democracy, particularly the trial and death of Socrates in 399 B.C. He came to believe that the only salvation was a philosopher turned king or a king turned philosopher. This belief was strengthened by his first journey to Italy and Sicily in 388 B.C., which also gave him Dion as a pupil. He continued his activities in Athens until he was invited by Dion to try and put his theories into practice in 367 B.C. We have now to ask what these theories were, not because Plato's experiment in Sicily was of great historical importance, but because of the influence Plato has had on later political thought and because Plato's foundation of the Academy is for us the beginning of organised Higher Education.

Although the Academy was not founded until 387 and may have owed a considerable amount to the Pythagorean schools in South Italy which Plato visited on his first westward journey, Plato certainly started writing and therefore presumably teaching in the first ten years after Socrates' death. His first aim was to preserve Socrates' teaching ; his second to develop it ; it is impossible to draw a fast line between the two stages, but the idea of a formal school, the Academy, marks as complete a breakaway from Socrates' informal conversations as from the lectures and instruction given by the travelling sophists. In his first works Plato wanted to give the flavour of Socrates' conversation on a particular occasion and the setting is as carefully drawn as it would be in a play : the *Apology* and *Crito* (which have been used above as evidence for Socrates' own life and thought) belonged to this first period.

The *Gorgias*, which includes Callicles' defence of the power politics (see above, p. 61), was written just before or just after Plato's first visit to Sicily in

388 B.C. ; here Socrates is in conflict with the professional orators who write speeches for politicians and teach them to speak. In one passage (464–5) Socrates develops the analogy between medicine and statesmanship which we have already noticed. He says that there are two arts or professions (*technai*) which work for the good of the body—gymnastics and medicine ; corresponding to these there are two arts which work for the good of the soul (both comprised in what he calls " statesmanship "—*politike*), lawgiving and justice (*dikaiosyne*) : " these four always care for the soul and the body so that they may be the best possible ". Four kinds of flattery correspond to these four arts ; they pretend to be the real thing but in fact only aim at giving pleasure, and are based on practice not on art ; they have no principles and no real knowledge of the people they serve : cookery corresponds to medicine, cosmetics corresponds to gymnastics, the flattery of the sophists corresponds to lawgiving, and rhetoric corresponds to justice. The cook knows nothing of what diet the patient needs but can tempt him with a meal that he likes. The beauty specialist knows nothing of the careful training which gives real health but can fake an appearance with rouge and powder. For Socrates and Plato, the political teaching of Protagoras and the speeches written by Gorgias are equally far removed from law-drafting based on the principles of true political theory and the justice administered by a judge in accordance with the law. Medicine, gymnastics, lawgiving, and justice are all professions or " arts " (*technai*) ; they are not purely *ad hoc* like the flatteries, but apply previously learnt principles to the particular case. Socrates demands the same kind of standards in the politicians.

Later Socrates asks Callicles (502e) what he thinks

of the rhetoric used on the Athenian people in the
assembly :

Do the orators [or politicians] seem to you to speak with
an eye on the ideal, aiming at making the Athenians as
good as possible by their speeches, or is their object to
indulge the Athenians ? Do they forget the common
interest for their private gain ? Do they play with people
as if they were children, only trying to indulge them and
not caring at all whether they make them better or worse ?

Callicles admits that this is true but suggests that
there could be a better kind of politician, whom Socrates
describes (504d) :

Will not the politician who is good and can really be
called a professional [*technikos* : as distinct from a flatterer]
have his eye fixed on modesty [*sophrosyne*] and justice and
adapt whatever words he speaks to their souls . . . always
considering how justice may arise in his fellow-countrymen's
souls and injustice be banished ?

The description recalls Thucydides' character of
Pericles (II, 65 : quoted above, p. 47) and probably
intentionally suggests that it is far from the truth,
because a few pages later Socrates asks Callicles
whether Pericles was by this standard a good citizen
(515c), because, if so, he should have improved the
citizens ; Socrates has heard that he corrupted the
citizens and made them idle, cowardly, talkative, and
greedy, by instituting payment for state services. His
reward was conviction for theft at the end of his life,
which would hardly have been his reward if he had in
fact treated them successfully like a good doctor. In
fact the modern cry for the good old statesmen of the
past is unjust (517b) ; the statesmen of the past knew
no more of statesmanship in the true sense than the
statesmen of the present ; they were only cleverer at

G

ministering to the people's desires and giving them harbours and dockyards and walls and tribute and suchlike nonsense (518c).

Besides the obvious criticism of the democratic imperialist policy, which might be expected from his aristocratic upbringing, Plato put forward here his own ideal of a statesman, worked out from Socrates' teaching and life as something superior to the politician of his day, just as in the *Protagoras* he had shown its superiority to the sophists. The true statesman must be a professional as the doctor is a professional. This implies first that he has knowledge, secondly that he is disinterested, and thirdly that his only object is the good of his subjects or fellow-citizens. The wise and good orator of Protagoras (see above, p. 49) goes a long way towards this, but lacks what for Plato is the most important element, the knowledge to decide what is good for his fellow-citizens.

The Academy was founded to train students in this knowledge, and both method and content are the subject of the *Republic*. The method is first suggested in the *Meno*, written soon after the first Sicilian journey, because in this dialogue Plato first shows his interest in mathematics. Mathematics is more than an analogy for the methods of pure thought, which are the essential background to true political thought, and there is ample evidence for close association between the leading Greek mathematicians of the time, such as Theaetetus and Eudoxus of Cnidos, with Plato's Academy.

In the *Republic*, which according to Jaeger was written in the years 375–370 B.C., although many of the ideas had been discussed by Plato far earlier—the philosopher king on the evidence of the *Seventh Letter* (see above) by 388 B.C., before his first Sicilian journey —Plato does not offer an immediate solution for the

troubles of fourth-century Athens ; what he does offer
is a standard, in the form of an ideal city, by which to
criticise all existing forms of constitution, although he is
clear that the ideal city cannot be realised : " perhaps
it is laid up in heaven as an example for him who is
willing to see it and seeing it to dwell there " (592b).
He also offers a method of education for the philosopher, who can in turn educate the whole city, and a
description of the philosopher's position in the city of
the fourth century.

The principle on which the ideal city is founded is
the natural differences of men : " each one of us is
born not entirely like the other but differing in nature
[*physis*], different people capable of different tasks.   Do
you not agree ? "   " I do."   " Would it therefore be
better for one man to ply many crafts or a single
craft ? " . . .   " Therefore more is produced better
and more easily when one man does one thing for
which he is suited, untroubled by other cares (370b)."
For Plato this principle is fundamental, as can be seen
from the fact that when he at last reaches a definition
of justice he defines it as the maintenance of this
principle " doing one's own job and not meddling
[*polypragmonein*] ".   It is the reverse of the Periclean
democratic ideal of versatility (see above, p. 45).
There are two elements, first that economic efficiency
can only be achieved by specialisation, and secondly the
natural differences between people.   Plato's principle
is therefore grounded in nature (*physis*) just as firmly
as is the sophistic rule of the stronger.   The interpretation of nature is different because it includes the
element of heredity seen not only in the professions
(the rhapsodes are " sons of Homer " and the doctors
" sons of Asclepius ") but also, of course, in aristocratic
families (see above, p. 26).   So the Platonic state

consists of four breeds (rulers, soldiers, farmers, craftsmen) and, like Theognis before him, he fears most a
mixing of the breeds (see above, p. 25). He knows,
however, that complete uniformity of breed is extremely
difficult to attain ; the children are inspected carefully
and if a child supposedly of one breed is found to be
in fact of another, he is immediately transferred to the
appropriate class ; in this sense equality of opportunity
is maintained. In the ideal state everyone is, according to his capacity, an expert and his life is directed by
the supreme expert, the philosopher king ; the general
qualities of respect and justice, which for Protagoras
make the citizen a valuable member of the legislature,
for Plato serve to keep him within his class.

Here is a fundamental distinction in theory between
the Periclean democracy and the Platonic ideal state.
Pericles trusts to free competition in all walks of life
to bring to the top the best people, the people who have
most *arete* (excellence in that particular sphere) ; in
the work of government these people produce the
plans, but the plans have to be approved by the
amateur judgment of the many who embody the
customs and traditions of Athens. In so far as there
is a political good it evolves from the interplay of the
officials' *arete* and the live tradition of amateur judgment. Plato believes in a knowable absolute good in
the light of which the philosopher king can plan the
whole administrative, economic, and educational
organisation of the state, giving the experts in each
profession, trade, or craft (*technai*) the framework
within which to work. In practice the immediate
contribution of the Academy to Athens was probably
a number of influential Athenians with trained minds
and a heightened sense of responsibility in official
conduct.

The ideal city is built on the principle of specialisation, and the defenders of the city are a special class, not a citizen army of amateurs (374b). In the fourth century the army became more professional, partly because of the increased specialisation in the technique of war under first Dionysius, then the Theban Epaminondas, and finally the Macedonians, partly because of the number of men prepared to enlist for pay in the service of other cities when an oligarchic or democratic revolution had forced them to leave their own. Plato therefore rejects the idea of a citizen army of amateurs, but emphasises the need of very careful training for these guardians, not so much in the art of war, which is obvious, as in the right attitude to their own city (376c). This leads him to the education of the guardians from their earliest youth on a carefully defined curriculum devised by the most rigorous censorship of existing poetry, art and music, dancing, and gymnastics : " Do you not know that the beginning of every job is the great thing, particularly when the victim is young and tender ? For then more than at any other time he is moulded and takes on any shape that you like to stamp on him " (377b). " The guardhouse of the guards must be founded on poetry, art, and music," because a change in these arts never takes place without a change in the greatest laws of the state (424c–d). He accepts the condition that the child is influenced by everything that he sees and hears, and by his censorship faces the double difficulty of the breakdown of traditional religion and morality (see above, p. 58) and of the prevailing emotional realism in Greek art and poetry.[1]

Plato's fundamental assumption is the Idea of the Good : it is possible for the philosopher to learn to see

[1] On this see *Greek Interpretations*, 76 f.

the universe as a purposeful system or, in other terms, as the work of God. This theology he develops in greater detail in the tenth book of the *Laws*.[1] Reduced to principles which can be embodied in children's literature, it becomes " God is good and the cause of good ; God does not change." All educational material must conform to these principles and in the *Laws* (801d) Plato appoints a board to censor new poetry and make a suitable anthology of old poetry. The geographers and doctors had shown that, whether we like it or not, the child is conditioned by his environment. Plato saw that this conditioning was far too important to be left to the haphazard efforts of nurses, parents, and itinerant sophists, and makes the first great plea for state education. Because he believed that the philosopher could come to know the purpose of the universe and could apply this knowledge to everyday life, he felt justified in prescribing a rigorous censorship of the content of state education. He defines education in the *Laws* as " the leading of children to the theory which has been pronounced right by the law ".

Judged by the standards of this city, governed by rulers whose only interest is the good of the citizens and who have the wisdom to see that every citizen has the job best adapted to his peculiar character, the existing constitutions of Greece (and the types of individual character which correspond to these constitutions as the just man corresponds to the ideal state) are viewed in the eighth and ninth books of the *Republic* as a progressive decline. The first stage is the Cretan-Lacedaemonian " which is praised by many " (543c), including the circle in which Plato himself grew up. This state presents some of the characteristics of the

[1] See Taylor, *Plato*, 489.

ideal state, has some of its own, and heralds some of
the next stage—oligarchy. Thus (547d)

in the honour given to rulers and the abstinence of the
warrior class from agriculture, handicrafts, and trade in
general, in the institution of common meals, and in the
attention paid to gymnastics and military training—in all
these respects this state will resemble the former :

in other words these are the elements in the Spartan
constitution which Plato regards as admirable.

But in the fear of admitting wise men to power . . . and
in turning from them to passionate and less complex
characters who are by nature fitted for war rather than
peace . . . this state will be peculiar. . . . And such
men will be covetous of money like those who live in
oligarchies ; they will have a fierce, secret longing for gold
and silver which they will hoard in secret places, having
magazines and treasuries of their own.

These sentences are a measure of Plato's disapproval
of Spartan policy, particularly since the end of the
Peloponnesian War, and a prophecy of the disaster of
Leuctra which came soon after the publication of the
Republic.

The next stage is oligarchy, the constitution of many
Greek cities and the constitution imposed on Athens
after the revolution of 411 B.C. and again in an advanced
form by the Thirty Tyrants. In part the change from
the military timocratic state to oligarchy was a historical change—the shift of power in the seventh
century B.C. from the landed aristocracy to the merchant class (see above, p. 13).

And so at last [551a], instead of loving contention and
glory, men become lovers of trade and money ; they praise
and admire the rich man and put him in office and dis-
franchise the poor man . . . they next proceed to make a

law which fixes a sum of money as the qualification for citizenship . . . and they allow no one whose property falls below the amount fixed to have any share in the government.

Plato sees the following defects in such a constitution : first, wealth is no standard of skill in office—no one would think of choosing a pilot for his wealth ; secondly the city is divided against itself, the rich and poor are always plotting against each other ; thirdly (552)

a man may sell all that he has, and another may acquire all his property ; yet after the sale he may dwell in the city of which he is no longer a part, being neither trader nor artisan nor horseman nor hoplite but only called a useless pauper,

and this class breeds criminals.

Plato sees three elements in an oligarchy which lead to a democracy ; the large pauper class who form the fuel of revolution, the spendthrift sons of good families, who lead the revolution, and the luxury and degeneration of the wealthy, which makes revolution possible.

And then [557] democracy comes into being when the poor conquer, and kill some of the rich and banish others, and give the remainder a share in the constitution and public offices on a basis of equality and the offices are for the most part allocated by lot.

Its characteristics are freedom of speech and action, the variety of the inhabitants, and their disregard for all rules ; democracy " never considers from what pursuit of life a politician comes but honours him if he says he is well disposed to the multitude ". Here he repeats in summary form what he had already argued at greater length in the *Gorgias*. He goes on to describe

the advanced democracy in colours which can be
paralleled from Thucydides, Aristophanes, and the
conservative writer known as the Old Oligarch : [1]
(562d–563) loyal citizens who obey the government
are called slaves ; fathers fear their own sons ; metic
and foreigner are as good as citizens ; slaves bought
with money are as free as their purchasers ; the
government is in the hands of idle spendthrifts who
squeeze the money out of the richest class and give
enough to the workers to keep them happy ; the rich are
finally forced to resist and are branded as oligarchs, and
the poor then find a champion who becomes a tyrant.

The chances of the true philosopher being able to
live in such a world are minimal. In the first place
the cities refuse to listen to him ; secondly the philo-
sophic nature is very rare and very open to corruption
by the power of mob applause or criticism echoing
round the rocks of the assembly place (492b—here he
may be thinking of Alcibiades). The tiny number of
true philosophers left are either saved by exile (like
Dion of Syracuse) or by living in a small city or by
being too ill to take part in public affairs (496a).
These few

keep quiet and pursue their own affairs, standing aside
from the storming wind and rain under the shelter of a
wall, seeing the rest filled with lawlessness, contented if
they live their life here pure of injustice and unholy deeds
and leave it with a fair hope, in peace and good will.

Nevertheless there is the possibility that somewhere
or some time a perfected philosopher might be given
charge of a state, or a king become philosopher, and
then the ideal state could be realised (499c).[2]

[1] See above, pp. 71, 75, 63.
[2] Cf. Laws, 709c–710c, the possible combination of a young tyrant
with an expert lawgiver.

Plato then describes the further education of the rulers of the ideal city. His higher education is best understood as a development of the Socratic technique of question and answer under the influence of contemporary mathematical thought, which he first brought into his published works in the *Meno* ; the aim is to push behind the individual and particular to the general and universal. Mathematics proceeds from the sensible world to the world of pure number, pure shape, etc., because the object of mathematics is to find out the laws of number and shapes ; it has to use visible examples as aids to its reasoning, but, when it has proceeded from there to discover the laws of abstract number or pure shapes, it can apply its reasoning again to the world of visible things. Therefore the guardians can be educated in pure reasoning by learning arithmetic, plane and solid geometry, astronomy, and harmonics. These arts are a preparation for learning dialectic, by which it is possible to push beyond the unexamined hypotheses of these abstract sciences to the first principle, which is the Idea of the Good or the Purpose of the Universe, or in other terminology, which Plato later uses, God. " Dialectic then is the coping stone of the sciences [*mathemata*] and is set over them : no other science can be placed higher—the sciences have reached their end " (534e). In modern terminology, dialectic would probably cover logic, theory of knowledge, and metaphysics, from which ethics and politics would then be derived to form the principles of practical ruling. For after their education the philosophers are to hold practical offices in the state (539c).

This section of the *Republic* gives the programme of the Academy and is the first preserved programme of an institution for higher education. The essential principle appears to be that the higher administrators, which the Academy is designed to produce, should be trained in the methods of abstract thought, in seeing general laws behind particular instances. Plato restricts the subjects to arithmetic, plane and solid geometry, astronomy, harmonics, and finally dialectic, because, for the ancient Greek in his day, these subjects most obviously lent themselves to this treatment. We admit a far wider curriculum including Arts subjects in our Universities, and Plato would doubtless approve, provided that his principle was preserved and the particular facts of each subject taught as a means to apprehending the general principles behind them.

When Dionysius the Elder died in 367, Plato, with the heart-burnings which he describes in the Seventh Letter, took his opportunity and accepted Dion's invitation to come to Syracuse and start the education of Dionysius the Younger. The education started, but Dion was accused by his enemies of aiming at tyranny for himself and was banished, probably before the end of 366 B.C. How much the opposition was frightened by Plato's doctrines, which would undermine the livelihood of those who lived on the tyranny, it is not possible to say. Dion went to Athens and Plato stayed on for a time in Syracuse attempting to bring about the recall of Dion. Plato paid a further visit to Syracuse in 361 B.C., more out of loyalty to Dion than in the hope of doing any real good with Dionysius, but his visit was quite useless. The further story of Dion's return in 360 B.C. and expulsion of Dionysius, the continued disturbances in Syracuse including the murder of Dion in 354 B.C., the return of Dionysius in 347 B.C., his surrender to Timoleon in 344 B.C., and the restoration of a modified form of democracy in Syracuse does not concern us.

Plato's attitude changed somewhat in his later years. The possibility of the philosopher king seemed even more remote than before the Sicilian experiment. When he wrote the *Politicus* (294 ff.) he still believed in the rule of the wise king who applies his art like a doctor for the good of the state, but doubted whether such a man could ever be found. Written laws and traditions are no substitute for the wisdom of the expert, which can deal flexibly with each particular case. But the perfect state with the philosopher king is an ideal, and existing forms of constitution are better or worse copies of it, just as all particulars are copies of their general concept. It is possible, however, that the laws and traditions of a city may be a fairly close copy of the ideal and are likely in any case to be better than the improvisations of a democracy, oligarchy, or tyranny. Therefore the prime division of constitutions is into law-abiding and lawless. Within the law-abiding groups monarchy is the best because the nearest to the ideal state, then aristocracy (in the sense of the rule of the few best), then democracy, in which knowledge and authority is most widely dispersed and therefore least effective. The same dispersal of authority makes democracy the most endurable of the lawless constitutions ; oligarchy comes next, and tyranny last.

He has changed the scheme of the *Republic* in several ways : the ideal state stands outside the series as an ideal and law-abiding monarchy takes its place at the head of the series (he may be thinking partly of the early days of the Persian empire as popularised in Xenophon's *Cyropaedia* and which he himself praised in his last work, the *Laws* (697) ; partly of the smaller monarchies, e.g. Evagoras of Cyprus and Hermias of Atarneus, on which see below). He has transferred

oligarchy from the law-abiding to the lawless constitutions (perhaps he is thinking of the Thirty in Athens).
He has put democracy above oligarchy and distinguishes two forms, law-abiding and lawless. This
can be interpreted by a passage in the *Laws*. The
Athenians, he says there (698–700), who met the
Persian invasion, were ruled by a kind of respect
(*aidôs*), which made them contented to live in slavery
to their laws—this is the law-abiding Athens of Aeschylus, and Plato distinguishes it sharply from the lawless
Athens of Pericles, which he characterises as unkindly
here as in the *Republic*.

The law and traditions which may be a close copy
of the ideal could be provided by the Academy and we
know instances where members of the Academy were
called in to provide new constitutions. Plato himself
in the *Laws* drew up the laws and constitution of a
city, which, unlike the city of the *Republic*, he thought
could be realised. Here he is considering the city as
a whole, whereas in the *Republic* he had concentrated
on the guardians and their education. He sketches
a city which, unlike the city of the *Republic*, he regards
as capable of realisation. It is a small, self-supporting
agrarian city of 5,040 families (737c) : the greatest
possible variation of wealth is to be from one to four
(744c). They are to be governed by 37 Guardians of
the Law (who must be over fifty years old and retire
at the age of seventy) and a representative chamber of
360 members elected for a year ; one of the Guardians
of the Law is elected Minister (*epimeletes*) of Education
for five years.

It is easy to brand Plato as a totalitarian and to stress
the censorship of literature, the ruthless suppression of
free thought in religion, the constitution thought out in
detail by a philosopher and imposed by a tyrant. This

was Plato's answer to the full Athenian democracy ;
half a century of full democracy had resulted in the
tyranny of Critias and the condemnation of Socrates.
Such a price was heavy to pay for unfettered individualism and free thought. It was possible, he thought, to
train people to know the truth about the universe
(which was later called philosophical theology) ; those
who were so trained had two complementary tasks :
to prescribe the moral and political laws within which
men should live, and to prescribe the elementary training which would fit men to live according to these laws.

In his old age Plato reiterated the fundamental
ideal with which he was inspired by Socrates—the
good life directed by wisdom, modesty, justice, and
courage. His political lifework was to try to realise
this on a large scale ; the short cut of converting
Dionysius the Younger into a philosopher king proved
impracticable. Two longer ways were practicable ;
one was to draw up the rules for a state education
which should teach children from birth not merely to
be brave as in Sparta, but also to be modest and just
and ready to receive wisdom when they were old
enough ; the other was to start the Academy as a
training in the abstract theory of virtues, which must
underlie all practical legislation.

IX

ISOCRATES AND DEMOSTHENES

ISOCRATES was born in 436 B.C., nine years before
Plato, and died in 338 B.C., nine years after Plato ;
his father, Theodorus, owned slaves skilled in the trade
of flute-making. He may have had some acquaintance
with Socrates in his youth (the only evidence appears
to be Plato, *Phaedrus*, 278–279e) ; [1] he is also said to
have known among others Protagoras and Theramenes.
Like Plato, Isocrates also saw his world smashed at
the end of the fifth century. Theramenes had been
put to death and his own patrimony had been lost in
the revolution. He made money by writing speeches
for the law-courts. By 392 B.C., he was able to set up
his own school and a year or two later put out his
manifesto in the speech *Against the Sophists* (XIII),
which, like all Isocrates' speeches, was a pamphlet to
be read and was never actually spoken. Some forty
years later Isocrates defined his position further in the
Antidosis (XV, 271) :

Since human nature [*physis*] does not permit us to have
scientific knowledge [*episteme*—the kind of knowledge that
Plato claimed to teach] of what should be done or said, I
consider those wise who in their opinions [*doxa*—which
Plato only uses of sense perception and never of reasoning]
for the most part light upon what is best, and I consider
philosophers those who spend time on studies which will
give them this kind of wisdom. . . . [276] Anyone who
purposes to write or deliver speeches which will command
praise or honour will not choose unworthy, trivial subjects,
or those only concerned with private business, but great,

---

[1] See *Greek Interpretations*, 71 f., on this and in general on Isocrates'
relation to Plato.

honourable and generous themes about state affairs. If
he does not find these, he will not achieve his objects. Of
the themes which contribute to his subject he will choose
the most relevant and attractive. The habit of surveying
these and assessing them will give him the power of dealing
with other themes besides the particular speech on hand
so that wisdom as well as eloquence falls to the lot of
those whose approach to speech writing is conditioned by
philosophy and ambition . . . [289] they despise pleasure
when of an age at which most men desire pleasure, and
when they could spend nothing and be idle, they prefer
to pay money and toil, and in their early youth they know
—what many older men have failed to learn—that to
manage one's youth rightly and honourably and to make
a good beginning in life, attention must be paid to oneself
rather than to one's possessions, and one must not strive
or seek to rule over others before finding a pilot for one's
own mind nor rejoice or be proud at any goods before
those which are born in the soul from education. . . .
[292] Those who are good orators by nature or chance
do not have the highest standards but usually speak as
chance demands, whereas those who have achieved this
power by philosophy and reasoning say nothing without
consideration and less often give bad practical advice.
Therefore all should wish for a large number of educated
orators, and especially you [the Athenians]. For your
superiority which distinguishes you from other countries
does not consist in military science nor in the goodness of
your constitution or the continuity of your ancestral laws
but in that which distinguishes men from other living
creatures and Greeks from barbarians ; you are better
educated than the rest in thought and its expression.

He had made much the same point thirty years
earlier in the *Panegyricus* (IV, 47 f.) :

Our city has so far surpassed the rest of mankind in
wisdom and its expression that her disciples have become

the teachers of the world, and the name of Greek no longer denotes a race but a kind of intellect and men are called Greek rather because they share our education than because of community of blood.

Pericles had called Athens an " education for Greece ", and the sophist Hippias of Elis had said that all wise men were kinsmen and friends and fellow-citizens by nature. With the schools of Plato and Isocrates this fifth-century dream had been further realised, but its continuance still seemed at that time to depend on Athens' political position in the Greek world and Isocrates believed that his school trained statesmen worthy of her traditions.

Isocrates made two claims for his school : it taught style and it taught the choice and arrangement of subject matter. His was a middle course between the orators (like Lysias), who only taught style, and Plato, who only taught, according to Isocrates, the most rarefied methods of pure thought. No less than Plato's dialogues, Isocrates' speeches were a new phenomenon in Greek literature for which it is difficult to find a modern analogy. Plato's dialogues might be compared to the most popular works issued by a University school of philosophy ; Isocrates' speeches to pamphlets on current affairs issued by a training college for statesmen run by a political party of the centre. Both Plato's school and Isocrates' school provided a permanent higher education in Athens and both men were Athenians, whereas in fifth-century Athens such instruction had only been provided by itinerant sophists.

A brief survey of some of the more important of his pamphlets will show both the leading ideas of Isocrates and the kind of education that he provided.

Isocrates thought that a common Greek culture

centred on Athens must be based on a unified Greek world also centred on Athens. This idea meant much more to him than to Plato, but Plato in the *Republic* makes quite different rules for war between Greeks and war between Greeks and barbarians ; war between Greeks he calls *stasis*, the word usually used for revolutions within a single city ; he also felt that the essential kinship between Greek states demanded a special international behaviour. Twice before Greece had been united, in the Trojan War and in the Persian Wars, and this memory survived. To the Athenian of the fourth century, the great days of Greece were the days of the Persian Wars ; if Greece could join in another crusade against Persia, Greece would be unified and the continuous wars between Greek cities with their accompanying internal revolutions might cease. The peace of Antalcidas in 386 B.C. acknowledged the supremacy of the Persian king over the Greek cities in Asia Minor, and in 380 B.C. Isocrates published the *Panegyricus*, in which he called " upon Athens and Sparta to forego their jealousies and to take the joint leadership of an expedition to Asia ",[1] or, as he himself put it later (XV, 57), disputed the right of the Lacedaemonians to take the lead. The inspiration is undoubtedly the idea of *Homonoia* (3) : if the warring Athenian parties could agree for the ideal of a free Athens, cannot the warring Greek states agree for the ideal of freeing the Greek cities of Asia ? Athens has the right to lead ; the keynote of her policy from the time of the discovery of agriculture has been to help mankind (28). She has welcomed strangers (41). She provides festivals and beauty for all comers at every season (46). Greek culture is Athenian culture (47). The Athenian empire was a rule of law over

---

[1] Jebb, *Attic Orators*, II, 18.

unanimous allies (104). Here Isocrates is trying to re-create the Athenian empire on a basis of consent with Sparta and her allies as willing partners (16). He did not achieve his full object ; on the other hand the Second Athenian League, which was formed in 378 B.C. to prevent " fresh inroads on Greek autonomy by Sparta ", probably owed something to the publication of the *Panegyricus*.

In the 370s, while Isocrates' pupil Timotheus was successfully conducting the naval warfare of the League, another pupil, Nicocles, succeeded his father Evagoras as king of Cyprian Salamis. Isocrates wrote three speeches, II *Nicocles*, IX *Evagoras*, III *ad Nicoclem*, in which he extols the two Cyprians as champions of Greek civilisation on the most easterly outpost of Hellenism against the Asiatic power of Persia, and prescribes the theory and practice of kingship. Plato had been talking about the philosopher king for something like twenty years when these speeches were written. Nicocles had been trained by Isocrates and Isocrates praises him as the first and only king to have undertaken the rigorous training of philosophy (IX, 78). He thinks that the educated monarch is the most likely of all governments to realise the ideal of government, which is that men shall have rewards according to their merits (III, 14). The education of the king benefits both the king and his subjects ; they get more kindly treatment and his rule has a safer foundation (II, 8). Isocrates hoped that Nicocles would realise on a small scale Protagoras' picture of the ruler who is " a blameless steward " for his people (see above, p. 49).

For Athens itself the solution could not lie in monarchy and in the *Areopagiticus*, which Professor Jaeger [1]

[1] *Paideia*, III, 110.

dates to the period before the Social War of 357 B.C.,
Isocrates pleads for the re-establishment of the Areopagus as a guardian of morality and a return to the
democracy of the period before the Persian Wars.
During the same period Plato was taking up the more
kindly attitude to democracy and particularly the
early Athenian democracy which we have noted in the
Politicus and *Laws*.[1] Isocrates was developing a theme
which he had stated more than twenty years before
in the *Panegyricus* (IV, 75). The Areopagus had been
reduced to a murder court by Ephialtes in 461 B.C.,
its other functions were restored by the Thirty Tyrants
in 404 B.C. (probably there the influence of the moderate democrats and Isocrates' teacher, Theramenes, can
be seen) and immediately removed again by the
restored democracy. Isocrates says that the Athenians
have frittered away all the gains of the Naval Confederacy because they neither have, nor make any
effort to have, a constitution which can make the right
use of success (14) :

The soul of the city is its constitution [*politeia*], which
has the same force as wisdom in the individual. This is
the supreme counsellor which preserves the good and avoids
the bad. To this laws and statesmen and private individuals must conform, and the prosperity of the individual
depends on the nature of the constitution. . . . [16]
I can only see future dangers being averted and present
evils dispelled, if we are prepared to resume the democracy
for which Solon, the greatest of democrats, legislated and
which Cleisthenes restored when he expelled the tyrants
and brought back the people. . . . [20] The constitution established by the rulers of that time was in practice
as well as in name kindly in temper and shared by all the
citizens ; it did not educate the citizens to regard licence as

[1] Cf. Jaeger, *ibid.*, 237, and above, p. 101.

democracy, lawlessness as freedom, unrestrained criticism as equality in law, the ability so to act as happiness, but such men were hated and punished and all citizens improved and made more modest. A great contribution to the good government of the city was the recognition of the more useful of the two theories of Equality—one deals out the same to all, the other to each his due ; they disallowed as unjust the Equality which thinks that good men and bad men are worthy of the same, and preferred the Equality which honours and dishonours each according to his worth and founded their constitution on this, not appointing officers by lot from the whole citizen body but preferring the best and the most capable for each several task. For they hoped that the rest would become like those who were put in control of affairs . . . [26] they realised that it was right that the People, like a tyrant, should establish the offices and punish those who erred, and judge on disputed points, while those who have leisure and sufficient substance should look after public affairs as servants of the People and receive praise for just conduct and be contented with this honour and receive no pardon but the greatest penalties for bad management.

Although Isocrates' criticism of the full Athenian democracy repeats the familiar charges that we know from Plato, his solution is not nearly so radical as Plato's. Instead of insisting on the expert like Plato, Isocrates uses the vaguer term " the best and most capable ", who later become equated with " those who have leisure and sufficient substance " ; he also leaves the people the ultimate decision on policy. This is a development of the theory of balanced democracy quoted above (p. 74), " the rich are the best guardians of money, the intelligent could give the best advice, and the many would give the best judgment when they had heard the case " (Thuc. VI, 39). If it is justifiable to trace it a stage further back to Sophocles (*Ajax*, 158 :

" the small without the great are a tottering fortress :
the little would find his best support in the company
of the great and the great would be supported by the
smaller "), it presumably sprang from the circle of
Cimon and Thucydides, son of Melesias. There is an
echo of their more feudal world in Isocrates when he
says (32) :

The poorer citizens were so far from envying those who
possessed more that they cared for the great houses like
their own, thinking their happiness constituted their own
riches. Those who had wealth did not despise the less
successful but, regarding the disability of their fellow-
citizens as their own dishonour, came to the rescue of their
poverty, giving some farms at moderate rents, sending others
out as merchants, giving others capital for industry [cf.
Aristotle, Politics, 1320a, 22].

The essential cause of this good constitution Isocrates
found in the establishment of the Areopagus to look
after the " good order " of grown-up citizens (37) :
" no one could take part in it except those who were
well born and had displayed much virtue and modesty
in their lives ". This council realised that " justice in
the soul was a surer sign of a good constitution than a
colonnade inscribed with many laws " (41). (It will
be remembered that in Plato's Gorgias the sphere of
legal justice is sick souls just as the sphere of medicine
is sick bodies.[1])

With this in mind they did not first consider the methods
of punishing the unruly but means of providing that they
should not commit crimes that needed punishment. They
considered particularly the younger citizens. They saw
that they were the most liable to disturbance and laboured
under the most varied desires [cf. Plato's account of

[1] Cf. also Rep. 425a ; Isocrates, IV, 78 ; Demosthenes, XX, 93 ;
XXVI, 26.

democracy in the *Republic*] and their souls most needed education by noble pursuits and pleasant tasks, only these would hold men brought up in freedom and accustomed to high thoughts.

Accordingly they turned the poor into farmers and traders and the rich to athletic competitions and hunting and philosophy (in Isocrates' sense) (46) :

Nor did they disregard the rest of their lives but divided the city into wards and the country into demes and watched the life of every man and brought the unruly before the Council. The Council gave warning to some, threatened others, and punished where it was right.

Isocrates diagnosed the same cause for contemporary evils as Plato, and however flagrantly the party school of political journalism differed in details from the university school of philosophy, both men prescribed moral education as the remedy. Both men, however, although they formed schools instead of entering practical politics, acknowledged the possibility of political education, although Plato, as we have seen, sometimes believed that his ideal City was stored up in heaven as a standard by which the just man could direct his life, but incapable of practical realisation. Isocrates describes his own position in several passages : in the *Panegyricus* of 380 B.C. (IV, 171) he says that " policy on the grand scale " has been left to him because he stands outside everyday politics, and he repeats much the same in his letter to Dionysius in 368 B.C. (*Ep.* I, 9). In the *Antidosis* of 353 B.C. he says that his associates have more leisure than anyone else in Greece (XV, 39) and complains that the Athenians are jealous of such people because they do not take office, although they serve the state by liturgies. He distinguishes himself from his teacher, the sophist

Gorgias, who had no taxes to pay because he always lived abroad.

The Cynics, on the other hand (the first great Cynic was Antisthenes, who was nine years older than Isocrates), based their doctrines on Socrates' asceticism and placed the highest values on an ascetic life with no ties in this world : they

led a life of formal mendicancy, without a house of their own, contenting themselves with the simplest food and the scantiest clothing . . . they attached no value to the opposition of freedom and slavery ; for the wise man was free even as a slave, and a born master ; for the wise man they considered civic life dispensable ; for he was everywhere at home, a citizen of the world [Zeller, *Outlines*, p. 110].

At the opposite pole was the philosophy of pleasure, preached by Aristippus of Cyrene, who was an exact contemporary of Isocrates. Both were philosophies for the private individual and not for the citizen ; so the " unmeddlesome man ", the *apragmon*, also became systematised in the fourth century.

The fact that these men found the good life impossible in the state is some measure of the discontent existing in the state. Plato vividly pictured the contemporary oligarchy as consisting of two hostile communities, the rich and the poor (p. 96, above). The same division existed also in fourth-century democracy ; Isocrates in the *Peace* (355 B.C.) and *Antidosis* (353 B.C.) speaks of the prejudices against the rich in Athens : [1] the politicians want to bleed the rich by contributions, liturgies, and lawsuits, so that all men may find equality in poverty (VIII, 124, 131) ; " to have the reputation of

[1] Cf. Demosthenes, X, 44 (341 B.C.), which allows a certain justice in the complaints of the rich.

wealth is more disastrous than to be caught red-handed in crime " (XV, 160, 164). The *Areopagiticus* gives something of the other side : the glaring contrasts of wealth when choruses can be produced in golden clothes and state-money spent on foreigners to row the fleet, while citizens need their jurors' obols for necessities and spend the winter in rags (54) : " now the number of the needy exceeds those with a competence, so that they may well be pardoned if they have no care for the state but only consider how to survive each day as it comes " (83). Rostovtzeff [1] thus describes the conflict between what he calls capitalism and state socialism in a democracy :

workshops of moderate size with a score of workmen, partly free and partly slaves, abounded in every large city. . . . The increasing amount of money gave birth to the banking industry and set credit transactions on a firm footing. . . . The slave markets provided slave labour in abundance ; and the growth of political anarchy increased the supply of slaves and lowered the price of labour. . . . Within each state capital had to fight the socialist tendencies of the government and its inveterate jealousy of all who, either by wealth or intellectual and moral superiority, rose above the general level . . . they [the rich] were compelled either to lend money to the state, or to undertake, at their own cost, the management of certain public duties, for instance, the purchase and distribution or sale of corn. They were required also to fit out warships for service, and to pay and train choruses and actors for theatrical performances. Such public burdens were called liturgies.

The economic situation of Greece changed for the worse in the second half of the fourth century, and, in spite of a decreasing citizen population, due both

[1] *Orient and Greece*, 316 f.

to wars and revolutions, which caused losses to citizen population both by casualties and by expulsions (hence the unfailing supply of mercenary soldiers), and to the increasing tendency to restrict the size of families by exposing children, unemployment and famine was common in Greece in the late fourth century. Rostovt-zeff [1] finds the cause in increasing industrialisation with a shrinking market. The Greek cities themselves were too poor to do more than import food and pay their mercenaries. With a strong nationalist revival in Persia, Greek cities had to pay for their oriental imports in silver instead of goods. In South Russia, too, archaeology has shown an increase in locally produced pottery and tiles at this time and therefore also a decrease in imports from Greece ; the same tendencies can be seen at work in Thrace, Illyria, Pannonia, Italy, and Etruria. There was then an economic argument to back Isocrates' plea for a new Persian War which he had made first in the *Panegyricus*, then to Jason of Pherae, Dionysius of Syracuse, and Archidamus of Sparta ; Eastern markets and Eastern colonisation might thereby again become possible. When he wrote the *Panegyricus* in 380 B.C., Isocrates saw the Ionian migration at the time of the Dorian invasion as a safety valve of this kind (IV, 34).

When the Second Athenian League ended with the revolt of the allies in the Social War (357–355 B.C.), Isocrates abandoned for the time his Panhellenic and anti-Persian dreams and supported the peace ; he traced the origin of Athens' disaster to her imperialism and desire for naval supremacy : "for this has now brought us to confusion and destroyed the old demo-cracy, when our ancestors led the happiest lives of all the Greeks " (VIII, 64). He has given up the picture,

[1] *Social and Economic History of the Hellenistic Age,* 104 f.

which he drew in the *Panegyricus*, of the Athenian
empire as a great civilising force, and even remembers
the image of Athens as " a vain woman " coined by the
aristocratic opposition to Pericles (see above, p. 46) :
" authority is like a harlot who makes men love her
and then destroys them " (VIII, 103). His criticism
of the democratic politicians is as bitter as anything
in Plato : they have got rich at the people's expense
and they want the people to be poor because they can
control it by its need for the payment that comes from
law-courts and assembly (VIII, 48 f., 124 f., 129 f.).
He asks for piety, modesty, justice, above all for peace
—in other words for a Little Athens policy of self-
sufficiency (VIII, 26, 63) : this will not only remove
the intolerable burden of war taxation and losses
(VIII, 20) but " we shall see the city with double its
present revenues and full of traders, foreigners, and
resident aliens, who have now deserted it " (VIII, 21).
This speech, *On the Peace*, was in line with the policy
of Eubulus, who was in all probability responsible for
making peace with the allies and rejecting appeals from
the people of Rhodes and Arcadia, the former of which
might have involved Athens in war with Persia, and
the latter with Sparta. Eubulus was a member of the
board which controlled the Theoric fund, which consisted of sums allocated for distribution to the people
to enable them to attend public festivals. By ensuring
the security of these distributions, Eubulus became
sufficiently popular to carry through financial measures
which made it possible to build up the fleet again to
a strength of 300 triremes and to repair the dockyards
and fortifications. Some of the feeling of this period
can be perceived in a pamphlet on *Revenues*, probably
wrongly ascribed to Xenophon, which can be dated
to 355 B.C. The author states at the beginning that

Athens is suspected because the poverty of her proletariat causes her to behave unjustly towards her
allies ; he is going to abolish this by making her
self-sufficient.   First, he proposes to encourage resident
aliens by freeing them from military service, and then
they will take full advantage of the admirable trade
facilities provided by Athens.   Trade could be further
encouraged by building public buildings for traders
and by leasing to them state-owned cargo-ships.   But
Athens' chief source of income was the silver mines at
Laureion, and the writer advocates the buying of state
slaves to let out to prospectors and a state control to
encourage opening new diggings ; these measures he
believes will usher in a new period of peace and plenty.

Philip of Macedon came to the throne in 360 B.C.
We need not follow his campaigns in detail, his earliest
conquests were in Thrace and threatened the Athenian
corn route.   By 352 he was in control of Thessaly in
Northern Greece.   In 346 he was in Central Greece
and had been made a member of the Amphictyonic
Council.   The final clash came in 338, when Philip
decisively defeated the combined Athenian and Boeo-
tian armies at Chaeronea.   In 346 B.C. Isocrates
addressed Philip of Macedon :

Philip is summoned as a Greek and a descendant of
Heracles to levy war against Asia.   Either he will conquer
Persia or at least he will detach from it all that lies westwards of a line drawn from Cilicia to Sinope.   In either
case he will free the Asiatic Greeks and make new settle-
ments for the Greeks who are now homeless [Jebb, *Attic
Orators*, II, 19].

In this speech (V, 12) Isocrates has abandoned hope
of achieving his object by political pamphlets or in a
world governed by law, the persistent belief of Athenian

democracy ; his only hope is to choose a great champion, and Philip may be able to fulfil this role because,
whereas other great men are hampered by laws and
cities, he has the authority and wealth and power,
which can persuade and compel. According to our
cast of mind we may regard this attempt to purchase
unity, peace, and prosperity at the price of enslavement
to a semi-Greek king as a wise acceptance of the
inevitable or as treachery to the innermost soul of
Athens. Isocrates saw in Philip a leader who would
unite Greece in a Panhellenic league against Persia ;
others, like the orator Aeschines in Athens, accepted
Philip's money and played the part of a Macedonian
fifth column in Greek cities.

Demosthenes spent his political life, which started
in 355 B.C., fighting Philip, because he saw that conquest by Philip, just as much as conquest by Persia,
meant the end of the independent life of the Greek
city-state. The story of his long struggle cannot be
told here, but we may note a few passages in the
speeches of this professional politician in which his
criticism of Athenian democracy comes very near to
the criticism of Plato, Isocrates, and Aristotle. One
speech ends with a summons to the Athenian democracy
to be worthy of itself because its statesmen in any
case will say what the Demos wants to hear ; the
summons echoes Aristophanes' criticism of the democracy in the *Acharnians* and *Knights* some seventy years
before (see above, pp. 75, 76) and Plato's criticism
of the Athenian orators in the *Gorgias* (see above,
p. 88).

Speakers do not make you good or bad but you make
them whichever you will. You do not seek what they
want ; they seek what they think you desire. If your will
is good, all will be well. For either no one will say anything

foolish, or you will not listen to him and that will do him
no good [XIII, 36].

The theme is taken up again in 348 B.C. in the
Third Olynthiac (21 f.) :

I think it is the duty of a good citizen to put the safety
of the state before the popularity of his speech. I have
heard, as probably you have, that this was the manner and
temper of public utterances of orators in the time of our
forefathers, whom all speakers praise but few imitate, I
mean Aristides, Nicias, my name-sake, Pericles. Since
these orators have appeared who ask " What is your
wish ? What shall I propose ? How can I please you ? "
the good of the state has been sacrificed to present pleasure
and popularity and things like this happen [Philip's
attack on Olynthus], and they get the honours and you
the shame.

He then sketches the external history of Athens from
Aristides to Pericles, when orators did not seek the
favour and friendship of the mob as they do now (25) :

This was the character of the rule in Greece. You must
consider also their character in the city both in public and
in private. Publicly they gave us temples and dedications
of a beauty which has never been surpassed. Privately
they were so modest and loyal to the spirit of the constitution that, if any of you in fact know where Aristides,
Miltiades, or any of these great men lived, you can see
that his house is in no way more dignified than his neighbour's. Their great happiness arose from their conduct of
affairs which was marked by good faith towards other
cities, piety to the gods, and equality in Athens.

He then describes the disastrous failure to make use
of the opportunities offered by the Spartan reverses
of 371 B.C. (28) :

Your present politicians lost in peace all the allies that

we gained in war, and we trained against ourselves an adversary of the magnitude of Philip. . . . Cast your eye on those responsible for this policy. Some have converted their poverty into wealth, and their obscurity into nobility, some have made themselves private houses more imposing than public buildings, and the worse things have gone for Athens, the better things have gone for them. What is the cause of all this and why did everything go right then and wrong now? Because then the people was prepared to act and fight itself [instead of using mercenaries] and was master of the state and lord of all rewards, and each citizen was happy to receive honour or office or other reward from the Demos. Now the opposite is true, the politicians are lords of the rewards and everything is done through their agency, but you, the Demos, your sinews cut, your wealth and your allies taken away, have become servants and appendages, happy if they give you money for entertainments or show you a pageant, and, worst of all, you are grateful for what is your own. They have shut you up in the city and led you into their ways; they have made you tame and feed you. . . . [33] But if even now you got rid of these habits and were willing to fight and act in a manner worthy of yourselves, and to use your surplus money at home for your foreign needs, perhaps, perhaps you might win some great and perfect thing and be rid of these pickings which are like doctor's sops.

Demosthenes, probably consciously, cast himself into the role of Thucydidean Pericles and here was stirring the people to some semblances of their former glory. The picture of a wayward mob which will vote anything to an orator who will flatter it we know from Lysias, Plato, and Isocrates; Demosthenes, who is here himself pleading for popular support against Philip, paints also the other side, the selfishness of the rich who keep the mob quiet by festivals and shows while they amass their private fortunes, a theme he had already used in the speech *Against Aristocrates* in 352 B.C. (note particularly XXIII, 124, 207, 209). In the *Second Olynthiac* (II, 29) he describes the parties in Athens :

Before, your contributions were managed by boards, now, your politics are managed by boards. An orator is the leader of each and a general under him and the three hundred who will do the shouting. All the rest of you are allotted either to this party or to that. You must give this up and become lords of yourselves again, and make speech, policy and action the common privilege of all.

Here again he is appealing to the common responsibility of the people.

In the law-court speeches at the beginning of the fourth century, the leading ideas were *nomos* and *homonoia*. These two ideas echo again in Demosthenes' speeches. Athens more than any other city is subject to the rule of law (XXI, 150) ; the laws are the chief cause of the city's blessings and of its being democratic and free (XXIV, 5) ; the laws are imposed with the consent of the citizens for their benefit (XXIV, 76) ; and the only just and steady guardian of the laws is the will of the people (XXIV, 37). The belief in law here is as strong as before, but there is a slight though important shift of emphasis from obedience to the law to responsibility for maintaining the laws. The second idea, *homonoia*—the agreement between the classes in the state—has two developments both foreshadowed in Isocrates. The first is the " humanity " (*philanthropia*) of Athens : Isocrates had spoken of the constitution as " kindly in temper and shared by all the citizens " ; Demosthenes says that " pity, pardon, and all the attributes of freemen are inherent in the laws and the customs of the constitution " (XXII, 57) and that it

is " the character of the city to pity the weak and not
to allow the strong and powerful to commit *hybris* "
(XXIV, 171). Secondly, from the " agreement between the classes " comes Demosthenes' particular
interpretation of equality in the balanced democracy.
The Athenians are equal under the law (XIX, 296)
and have equal rights in the state ; above this basic
level there is free competition to serve the state (XXI,
67, 159) ; the rich are not grudged their wealth if
they are prepared to spend in the state's need (X, 44) ;
no one is compelled to take part in public service
(XIX, 99) but if he volunteers and is successful in
" the contest of the good " he is rewarded by his
peers (XX, 16, 107).

In democracy so conceived, the whole people has
its part to play. The idea of responsibility comes out
most clearly in the speeches on policy, e.g. in the
Symmories (XIV, 14) " first and greatest is that you
should make up your mind that every one of you is
going to be willing and eager to carry out whatever is
necessary " and in the *First Philippic* (IV, 47) " you
must see that the same people fight the campaigns,
witness the strategy, and sit in judgments at the audits
when they return, so that you do not only hear about
your successes and failures, but see them in person ".
Demosthenes substitutes the responsibility of the individual citizen for the education of statesmen. The
Athenian Demos was still capable of a response as
Chaeronea showed.

The citizen army of Athens was no match for the
professional army of Philip. When the battle was over,
Philip " guaranteed to Athens freedom from Macedonian invasion by land and sea, and left her in
possession of the chief of the islands of the Aegean—
Lemnos, Imbros, Delos, Scyros, and Samos " (*CAH*,

265).   The terms were far better than any that could
have been expected.   It is perhaps worth remembering
that Aristotle, who had lived in Plato's Academy for
twenty years until 347 B.C., had been the tutor of
Philip's son Alexander since 342/3 B.C. and therefore
it is reasonable to suppose that his memories of Athens
contributed something to Philip's clemency.

X

ARISTOTLE

ARISTOTLE'S father was a doctor to Amyntas II, king of Macedon, and he was therefore brought up at the Macedonian court, to which he returned many years later to be tutor of Alexander the Great. In 367 B.C., at the age of seventeen, he came to Athens to study under Plato, and only left Plato's Academy when Plato died in 347. He was therefore a student in the Academy when Plato was producing the later dialogues from the *Theaetetus* to the *Laws*. The early period dominated by Socrates' influence and the establishment first of the nature of the virtues and then of the theory of ideas was over ; and Plato was now more concerned with the methods of thought and the establishment of terminology than with political or ethical theory in itself. Plato made one more journey to Sicily in 361 B.C. and wrote the *Laws* before he died ; but if the rest of his published dialogues are any guide, the Academy became more a research institute than a training-ground for young politicians in the later years of Plato's life, and there Aristotle's ideal of the life of " pure contemplation " was formed. The legacy of the earlier period of the Academy was the idea of a Utopia as an essential part of political theory ; the legacy of the later period of the Academy was the ability to classify and analyse under general headings which are applicable not only to constitutions but to all phenomena. As Professor Jaeger has shown, the history of Aristotle's own political and ethical thought is largely the history of the penetration of the earlier idea by the later, until Aristotle emerged

finally in his second Athenian period as the father
and organiser of all knowledge.

On the death of Plato in 348/7 B.C., Aristotle left
Athens and settled with Hermias of Atarneus in Asia
Minor. He was evidently invited by Erastus and
Coriscus, two Platonic philosophers who had already
settled with Hermias, and had persuaded him to convert
his tyranny into a milder form of government ; Plato's
Sixth Letter is addressed to all three and commends this
ideal friendship between pure philosophy and practical
administration. Whatever reason Aristotle had for
leaving Athens (the most probable was that he was
too young to become head of Plato's Academy and too
original to remain subordinate to any head but Plato),
he went to a friendly community where political philosophy was being put into practice. In the next five
years the first versions of the *Politics*, *Ethics*, and *Metaphysics* were probably composed. Then (343-342 B.C.)
Aristotle went, possibly as an ambassador from Hermias,
who was allied with Philip against Persia,[1] to Philip
of Macedon and became the tutor of his son Alexander,
who was then fourteen years old.

What Aristotle taught Alexander, we do not know,
but we can guess a little.[2] There is a good tradition
that Aristotle was working on Homer at this time and
that Alexander, who claimed descent from Achilles on
his mother's side, and when he later invaded Persia,
posed as a second Achilles, learnt Homer from Aristotle.
We are apt to think of Achilles primarily as the first
tragic hero, a great nature, marred by the fault of
passionate anger, tragic because of his foreknowledge
that " death awaited him very soon after he had slain
Hector ". For Aristotle (and therefore for Alexander)
he was much more simply the young warrior who led

---

[1] Jaeger, *Aristoteles*, 120 f.   [2] See Tierney, *Studies*, 1942, 221 f.

the Greeks against the Eastern barbarians. The pro-
paganda line of the Persian expedition must have been
that Alexander was a second Achilles leading the
Greeks to conquer the barbarians, and this conception
tallied both with the earlier preachings of Isocrates
(see above, p. 114) and with the feeling at the court
of Hermias, who had been an outpost of Greek civilisation in the Persian Empire and was foully murdered
by the Persians in 341 B.C. ; in this spirit Aristotle
counselled Alexander to treat the barbarians as a master
and the Greeks as a leader, caring for the latter as
friends and kindred, but looking after the former as
he would animals and plants.[1] A quite different feeling towards Persia can be seen in other fourth-century
documents, e.g. in Xenophon's *Cyropaedia*, which
describes the old Persian education as something both
admirable and imitable, in Plato's discussion of the
Persian constitution in the *Laws* (697c), and in the
praise of early Persian religion in Plato's *Epinomis* and
Aristotle's *de Philosophia*. The growth of this kind of
feeling made possible Alexander's idea of uniting the
best of Greece with the best of Persia, which he put into
practice as soon as he had conquered Persia.

On his father's side, Alexander traced his descent
from Heracles, the hero who had been accepted by
the aristocrats in Athens from Solon's time as the
civiliser of the world and the type of discipline and
who, in the myth told by the sophist Prodicus in the
late fifth century, had chosen the life of virtue (*arete*)
in preference to the pleasurable life of vice. Aristotle
must have translated these heroic ideals into modern
political terms coloured by the fourth-century teaching
of Plato and Isocrates. Two passages in the *Politics*
sum up the political position of Alexander. The first

[1] Tierney, 228.

is where he recognises a form of kingship, analogous
to the government of a household by its master, which
may be kingship over a city or people or multitude of
peoples (1285b, 30). In the second he says that monarchy is right where the population is fitted by nature
to carry a family excelling in the virtue of political
leadership (1288a, 8). Here he has introduced the
very important principle that the form of government
may vary with the natural constitution of the people
(*physis*). It is an old idea, the interplay between *nomos*
and *physis*, which is found first in a Hippocratic treatise
of the fifth century and was probably also held by
Protagoras,[1] but does not appear again in this form
until Aristotle. Alexander himself adopted this principle when he organised his empire.

In 335/4 B.C. Aristotle returned to Athens and taught
at the Lyceum. Alexander died in 323 B.C. and anti-
Macedonian feeling flared up in Athens ; Aristotle
was charged with impiety and withdrew to Chalcis in
Euboea, where he died in the next year. Athens was
to be the university city of Alexander's empire and
Aristotle's school had Macedonian support. In one
instance we can perhaps see how Aristotle took pains
to fit his new school into the Athens of this time.
Lycurgus, the Athenian statesman, was concerned to
restore Athenian morale after Chaeronea and felt that
a return to the great days of the fifth century was
needed ; besides reorganising public cults and rebuilding temples, he rebuilt the theatre of Dionysus in stone,
set up in it bronze statues of the three great tragedians,
Aeschylus, Sophocles, and Euripides, and arranged for
official acting texts of their plays. Aristotle based his
dramatic theory in the *Poetics*, which he wrote at this
time, on the tragedies of the three great fifth-century

[1] Cf. Loenen, *Protagoras*, 113.

poets, and researched into the records of the Dionysiac festival ; he also defended classical tragedy against the strictures of Plato by insisting on its value as an emotional katharsis.

During this second residence in Athens, Aristotle compiled, or got compiled, accounts of 158 Greek constitutions (of which a single one survives, *The Constitution of Athens*), and on these Books I, IV, V, VI of the *Politics* are based. This part of the *Politics* has therefore a basis in historical research as complete as was possible at that time, and its importance for us lies in its being a codification of political practice during the whole period from Homer to Aristotle. Our purpose in examining the *Politics*, both the earlier books (II, III, VII, VIII), written while the influence of Plato was stronger, and these later books, is to pick out those passages where Aristotle is concerned with the various problems which we have seen arising in our survey of the Athenian democracy.

After a preliminary criticism of Plato's *Republic* and other theoretical and historical constitutions (Book II), Aristotle at the beginning of Book III defines constitution (*politeia*) as an arrangement of those who inhabit a city, and therefore presupposing the definition of a citizen. The essential qualification of a citizen he sees (1275a, 22), not in birth or property or parentage, but in the right to share in the judicature and the legislature ; his very terminology shows that he is here thinking of Athens, although he rejects the Athenian admission of artisans and mechanics to citizenship because they have not the leisure to practise virtue (1278a, 8). The great value of this definition is that it defines the citizen in purely political terms ; the citizen is a citizen because he does a certain job in the city, and this constitutes his real right to be a citizen.

Political science by this time has become separated from ethics, although still closely allied to ethics.

The purpose of the state is the common good of the citizens because it is derived from the family, in which the father rules over free men and women for their good ; the other primitive relationship, master and slave, serves the good of the master, not of the slave (1278b, 33). Therefore (1279a, 17) the true forms of constitution aim at the common good—they are monarchy, aristocracy (in which the " best men " rule), and what he calls " constitutional government " (*politeia*), in which a larger body rule, those who are qualified to bear heavy arms. There are three perversions of these types : tyranny, which aims at the tyrant's good ; oligarchy, which aims at the good of the wealthy ; and democracy, which aims at the good of the poor. Aristotle calls them perversions because their object is the good of the governor or governors, not the good of the whole citizen body ; they are extensions of the master/slave relationship and not of the father/family relationship. The six constitutions, three true and three perverted, are familiar to us from Plato's *Politicus* (see above, p. 100), but Aristotle has altered the basis of classification. Plato first divided constitutions into law-abiding and lawless, and then arranged each category in an order of merit. Aristotle's prime division is by their approximation to the relationship subsisting in the family and the relationship between master and slave. Both kinds of constitution have a basis in *physis* because they derive from these primitive natural relationships, and Aristotle makes no order of merit because the form of government varies with the natural characteristics of the people. Aristotle's " constitutional government " is perhaps a recollection of the 5,000 of 411 B.C., which Thucydides regarded as the perfect blend of oligarchy and democracy.

He therefore defines a city thus (1280b, 29) :

It is clear that a city does not imply merely sharing a locality nor is its object simply the avoidance of injury or the exchange of goods. These conditions must exist if there is going to be a city, but even if they all exist, that does not necessarily make a city, but the sharing of households and families in the good life, for the sake of a perfect and self-sufficient life . . . i.e. a life of happiness and honour. The political community must be defined as existing for the sake of noble action but not merely for community-living. Whoever contributes most to such a community, has a greater share in the city [i.e. is more truly a citizen] than those who have equal or greater freedom or nobility of birth but less political virtue or than those who are superior in wealth but inferior in virtue.

Here again Aristotle is close to Plato's *Politicus* and adopts Plato's standard, political *arete*, at the same time recognising that political *arete* is a much better criterion than aristocratic birth, oligarchic wealth, or democratic equality. Equality of opportunity means opportunity to show political virtue and to be rewarded for it and not the allocation of political offices by lot ; this had been recognised by Pericles and here Aristotle is in the Periclean tradition.

In the next passage Aristotle breaks right away from Plato and gives a philosophical justification for " the amateur judgment ", as it has been defined above in our discussion of Pericles and of the balanced democracy propounded by the Syracusan Hermocrates (pp. 51, 74). He does not accept Protagoras' solution that there are certain political virtues which every citizen may be expected to possess, but propounds instead a theory which implies a kind of corporate personality in the assembly and the jury (1281a, 39) :

The principle that the multitude ought to be supreme rather than the few best is capable of a satisfactory explanation and, though not free from difficulty, yet seems to contain an element of truth. For the many, of whom each individual is but an ordinary person, when they meet together, may very likely be better than the few good, if regarded not individually but collectively, just as a feast to which many contribute is better than a dinner provided out of a single purse. For each individual among the many has a share of virtue and prudence, and when they meet together, their moral and intellectual power works rather on the analogy of one man with many feet and many hands and many senses . . . [1281b, 21] if this is true, it would solve the problem of what authority to give the mass of free citizens, who are neither rich nor have any claim to virtue. For it is not safe for them to take part in the greatest offices (for their folly will lead them into error, and their dishonesty into crime), but to give them no share is dangerous (for when many poor men have no citizen rights, the city is full of enemies). It remains for them to share in deliberation and justice. Therefore Solon and certain other legislators give them the power of electing to offices and calling magistrates to account but they do not allow them to hold office singly. When they meet together their perceptions are quite good enough and combined with the better class they are useful to the state.

In answer to Plato's objection (*Laws*, 945) that election of magistrates and audit at the end of their term is the most important act of government and therefore ought to be done by the wisest citizens, Aristotle says (1282a, 34) :

The power does not reside in the juror or the councillor or the member of the assembly but in the jury and the council and the people. Each individual is only a part of these bodies . . . so that the many justly rule over the greater magistracies ; for the people, the council, and the courts consist of many persons and the sum of their qualifications is greater than the qualification of the one or few who hold great offices.

This passage reads rather as if Aristotle is somewhat unwillingly accepting a piece of Athenian democratic political theory. He also accepts the supremacy of the law (1282b, 1) : " laws when good should be supreme and the official, whether one man or many, should only decide where the law cannot speak precisely because it is not easy to make universal definitions about everything ".

Aristotle continues : every science and art aims at a good ; political good is justice, i.e. the common advantage. He defines the various kinds of justice in the *Ethics* (Book V). Political justice exists only between men whose mutual relations are governed by law and part is natural and part conventional ; by the latter Aristotle means all the different enactments in different states, by the former " that which everywhere has the same force and does not exist by people's thinking this or that " (1134b, 18). Thus, in answer to the sophists who had stressed the relativity of *nomos*, Aristotle posits also a universal justice, which is recognised everywhere and therefore has a wider sanction than the law of the particular city ; this conception clearly develops out of such earlier ideas as the divine law of the *Antigone*. " Political justice " therefore means what is prescribed by the law of a particular state. Justice also means abiding by these laws and so possessing the virtues which are necessary to keep the law and so " virtue in relation to one's neighbour " (1129b, 25) ; here Aristotle quotes the passage of Theognis expounded above (p. 25) and his definition

itself develops out of Plato's definition in the *Republic* :
" to do one's own job and not meddle ".

Aristotle further considers the principle by which
justice must be administered and distinguishes distributive justice, remedial justice, and justice in exchange.
The root principle is the old law of retribution, but the
application, particularly in distributive justice, leads
us back to political theory. Aristotle adopts what
Isocrates had called " the more useful of the two kinds
of equality . . . which honours and dishonours each
according to their worth " (above, p. 109). But in
accordance with his idea of political relativity the
" worth ", in proportion to which distribution of
offices, money, or other things are made among the
citizens, varies according to the constitution. The
standard of worth " is defined by democrats as freedom,
oligarchs as wealth, and aristocrats as *arete* " (*Ethics*,
1131a, 28) ; " but for good life, education and *arete*
would have the most just claim " (*Politics*, 1283a, 24).

All the standards work in practice in the different
sorts of constitutions, but all are open to the difficulty
that whatever standard is adopted logically the man
who approximates nearest to it should in justice be
ruler of all (1288a, 15) :

When a whole family or some individual is so superior
in virtue that his virtue surpasses the virtue of all the rest,
then it is just that such a family should be royal and in
command of all and that such an one should be king. For,
as has been said before, this is not only just according to
the justice which all writers of political theory recognise
whether aristocratic, oligarchic, or democratic (for they all
recognise excellence but not the same excellence) but
according to our former argument. For it is not suitable
to kill or banish or ostracise such a man or to expect him
to be part ruler, part ruled : for it is not natural for the

part to overshadow the whole and this would happen in
the case of such a superior person. So that the only thing
left is to obey him and make him master not in part but
absolutely.

Thus Aristotle gives the same answer as Aeschylus gave
in Aristophanes' *Frogs*, when asked about Alcibiades :
" It is best not to bring up a lion in the city. If you
do, you must subscribe to its behaviour " (see above,
p. 62). The reference to the three forms of constitution and to ostracism shows that Aristotle is not only
thinking of the Macedonian kings, nor can his words
be limited to a hypothetical philosopher king who might
or might not be accepted if he were ever born. But
he is also thinking of the problem of outstanding figures
in a democracy (in their different ways Antigone,
Socrates, and Pericles himself were examples) and says
in effect that special powers and special concessions
may sometimes be justified.

Aristotle then considers his ideal state. He first
considers what is the most desirable life for the individual and then argues, like Plato in the *Republic*, that
this life is the same for the commonwealth as for the
individual (1323b, 21) :

Each one has just so much of happiness as he has of
virtue and wisdom and of action according to these . . .
it follows that the happy city is that which is best and acts
honourably . . . neither man nor city can do anything
honourable without virtue and wisdom. The courage,
justice, and wisdom of a city have the same force and form
as the qualities participation in which justify an individual
being called just and wise and modest.

This of course is a repetition of the standpoint of
Plato's *Republic*. Aristotle then raises the question of
whether the life of the virtuous individual includes

political activity or not (1324a, 26) : " whether one should choose the life of political activity or rather the life which is free of all external things, a life of contemplation, which alone, according to some, is the life of philosophy ". The latter view was the view of the Cynics (see above, p. 112), and we have had occasion to notice the gradual tendency of the *apragmon* to draw away from political life (see above, pp. 45, 68). Aristotle answers (1325b, 14) :

If we can assume that happiness is virtuous activity the active life will be the best both for the city collectively and for individuals. But the active life need not necessarily have relation to others, as some think, nor are those ideas only to be regarded as practical which are pursued for the sake of practical results but much more those which contain their own end and the pure activity of contemplation and thought.

Here he puts the active life and the contemplative life on a level ; later in his second Athenian period he regarded the life of pure contemplation as superior to the life of activity, and the breach between the scholar and the citizen became more obvious.

He next considers the size of the perfect city (1326a, 35) :

There is a limit to the size of the city as in everything else, animals, plants, implements. . . . The city which is too small is not self-sufficient (and the city should be self-sufficient) and the city which is too populous is self-sufficient in the necessaries of life but is like a nation and not a city. For a constitution can hardly exist in it. Who will be a general when the multitude is so excessive or who a herald without the voice of Stentor ? A city must therefore have sufficient population to make it self-sufficient for a good life according to the standards of a political community. . . . How far it may exceed this is easy to see.

For both rulers and ruled have activities ; the special functions of the ruler are to command and to judge. To judge in the law-courts and distribute offices according to worth the citizens must know each others' characters, as where this is impossible both the choosing of offices and the decision of lawsuits is bound to go wrong. For extemporisation which is clearly necessary in an excessive population is unjust. Also it is easy for foreigners and resident aliens to take part in the city's business : for it is not difficult to escape notice because of the excessive size of the population.

The aim of happiness, defined as virtuous activity, needs leisure for its achievement, but all the citizens are to be capable of achieving it ; it follows therefore (1328b, 39) that " the citizens must not live the life of mechanics or tradesmen (for such a life is ignoble and inimical to virtue) nor must they be farmers ; for they need leisure both for the development of virtue and the performance of political duties ". Therefore the ideal city has a citizen body of soldiers (the younger citizens), rulers (the soldiers in their later years), and priests (the oldest citizens). This subsists on a slave population of farmers, craftsmen, labourers, and tradesmen. The citizen body is to be composed of good men (1332a, 31) :

for a city to be virtuous is not a matter of luck but of knowledge and will. . . . The next question therefore is how a man becomes virtuous [1332a, 35]. . . . [1333a, 11] Since we say that the virtue of the statesman (πολιτικοῦ) and ruler is the same as that of the best man and that the same man ought to be a subject earlier, and a ruler later, the lawgiver must see that they become good men and the methods of achieving this and what is the aim of the best life.

The soul is divided into two parts ; the Reason and that which is capable of listening to Reason (1333a, 30) :

The whole of life is divided into two parts, business and leisure, war and peace, and all actions into those which are necessary and useful and those which are honourable. All these points the statesman should keep in view when he frames his laws ; he should consider the parts of the soul and their functions and above all the better and the end. In the same way with regard to their lives and their choice of activities. Men need to be able to be busy and make war ; still more to be at peace and have leisure ; men need to do the things that are necessary and useful but still more to do the things that are honourable. To this end they are to be educated when they are still children and at other ages in so far as they need education.

Before turning to some passages in the books of the *Politics* which were composed during Aristotle's later Athenian residence, let us compare Aristotle's political philosophy with Plato's. First, Aristotle accepts and includes in his theory accomplished facts such as the Athenian democracy and the possibility of a reasonable life in it, which Aristotle himself as well as Plato had experienced, and the outstanding excellence of Philip and Alexander of Macedon, which makes it necessary to allow them quite special powers. Secondly, he enumerates all the different elements in the state and concedes their right to exist. Thirdly, the citizen *quâ* citizen has a certain kind of life in a city and Aristotle firmly bases his theory on that ; the aim of life in a city is the common good of the citizens, i.e. their happiness. To be happy they must have the chance of virtuous activity, which in its political aspect consists in being ruled and ruling, whereas in Plato's ideal state nobody rules except certain very carefully selected guardians. Fourthly, virtuous activity, which is Aristotle's definition of happiness, is impossible without leisure, and therefore Aristotle perfectly logically confines the citizenship to the classes that have leisure ; the possibility of the working classes having leisure did not occur to him, because in the absence of machinery there was no such possibility in ancient Greece ; given the conditions of fourth-century Greece, he has done the best he can to provide an ideal state for the greatest possible number, where Plato, in the *Republic*, sacrificed every class in the state to the guardians. Fifthly, although his city as a whole may be ideal and incapable of realisation, the ideal of policy which he puts before his statesman is perfectly real and of general application : he sees as clearly as Plato that the virtue of the citizens depends on education in the widest sense and that everything included under the Greek word *nomos* must be directed to this end.

In the fourth book of the *Politics* (1295a, 25) Aristotle draws another city :

the best constitution and the best life for most states and most men, neither assuming a standard of virtue which is above ordinary persons, nor an education which needs exceptional favour from nature or circumstances, nor an ideal state which is an aspiration only, but having regard to the life in which the majority are able to share, and to the form of government which states in general can attain. . . . In all cities there are three parts of the city, the very rich, the very poor, and the third which is the mean between them. Since it is admitted [in the *Ethics*] that moderation and the mean are best, it is clear that it will be best also to possess the gifts of good fortune in modera- tion. For thus obedience to reason is easy, but it is difficult to listen to reason either if one greatly excels in beauty, strength, birth, or wealth, or at the opposite end of the scale if one is excessively poor or weak or has practically no part in the privileges of citizen life. For the former become violent and great criminals, and the latter rogues and petty criminals. The one sort commit offences from

K

violence [*hybris*], the other from villainy. Moreover those who have too much of the goods of fortune, strength, wealth, friends, and other such things, neither like nor understand being subjects (and this comes from their earliest youth ; for luxury makes them unused to obeying their teachers) and those who are excessively poor are too humble. So that the very poor do not know how to rule but understand being subjected to a regime of slavery, while the rich are not prepared to be subjected to any rule but to rule as masters. It is therefore a city of slaves and masters but not of free men, and of envious slaves and proud masters. This is far removed from friendship and political community ; for community implies friendship. Enemies are not even prepared to share the same path. A city wants to be composed of people who are like and equal as far as possible [hence the violent restriction of the franchise in the ideal city], and these qualities are found particularly in the middle class. Such a city necessarily has the best political life because it is formed of what we call the natural elements for the constitution of the state. And the middle class are the most secure in a state. . . . It is clear that the best political community is based on a middle class and those states are likely to be well administered in which the middle class is large and larger, if possible, than both the other classes or at any rate than either singly. For the addition of the middle class turns the scale and prevents excesses on either side. Therefore it is the greatest good fortune that the members of the citizen body should have a moderate but sufficient substance as, when some possess great wealth and others nothing, the result is either extreme democracy or pure oligarchy, or a tyranny as the result of either extreme ; for a tyranny may arise from the most revolutionary form of democracy or from an oligarchy, but much less from a middle and nearly equal condition. . . . That the middle is best is clear. For it alone is free from faction and where the middle class is large there are least likely to be conspiracies and schisms among the citizens.

The emphasis on the middle class has both a philosophical and a historical justification. The Greek word for " middle " is also used for a mathematical " mean " and in Aristotle's philosophy every virtue is a " mean " between two extremes ; justice itself is a " mean " ; the city must neither be too large nor too small, and the work of art must neither be too large nor too small. Poet after poet from the seventh century onwards prays to be a middle citizen, " neither a sacker of cities nor a slave captured in war ", and the virtue of modesty (*sophrosyne*) is often preached in such terms as " say nothing big ", " nothing too much ". Aristotle is therefore developing a very old strain in Greek thought. Historically we have noticed again and again that the troubles of Greek city life were due to the sharp cleavage between the rich and the poor—in Solon's account of early Athens, Thucydides' discussion of revolutions, and Isocrates' description of conditions in the fourth century.

The great evil of Greek politics in the late fifth century and early fourth century was the instability of the democracy in Athens and the depredations of the oligarchs whenever they had power. The instability of the Athenian democracy Aristotle ascribes (1293a, 1) to the payment of offices (see above, p. 43) : where offices are paid, the poor citizens, who have no education and therefore are at the mercy of any demagogue who flatters them, have the most leisure and therefore the state is governed by the poor, who are a majority, and not by the laws ; he defines this as a rule of *psephismata* (the day-to-day decrees of the assembly) as contrasted with the rule of *nomos* (law) (1292a, 2 ff.). In the older Athenian democracy of the days of Solon and Cleisthenes, Aristotle, like Plato and Isocrates (see above, pp. 101, 108), saw a respect for law (the idea may be phrased as respect for *nomos* or as *sophrosyne* or as *aidôs*), which he attributes to the moderate form of democracy in contrast to the full-blown democracy of Periclean and later days ; this democracy he describes thus (1292b, 25) :

When the agricultural element and those who possess moderate substance have the supreme power in the constitution, they govern according to the laws. They have to live by their labour and have no leisure ; therefore they put the law in command and only attend the necessary assemblies. . . . [1318b, 27] It is advantageous and customary in this form of democracy that all should elect to office and hold scrutinies [*euthynai*] and sit in the law-courts, but that the greatest offices should be filled up by election and from people having a property qualification, the greater requiring a greater qualification, or if property qualifications are not required, then they must elect those who have capability. Such methods of government are bound to be good (for the offices will be held by the best men and the people will be willing and will not envy the nobles, and the nobles and the aristocrats will be satisfied with this arrangement).

In the earlier Athenian democracy the initiative lay with those who had the leisure and the capacity to use it ; their use of it was controlled by the common sense of the ordinary citizen. Both parties in the state regarded the *nomos* as supreme and the prime function of the ordinary citizen was to see that government was in accordance with the *nomos*, the living tradition of Athens.

The value of Aristotle for us lies in the penetration and detachment of his political thought. His premises that the state exists for the common good of the citizens and that the good of the citizens consists in the happiness of virtuous activity (including the life of contemplation) are premises which we should accept. His conclusions are in part vitiated for us because he could not foresee the good and evil brought by machinery and improved communications, but these are factors of error which can be assessed, nor is it impossible in some cases to apply the corrective. Living as a wanderer now in Athens, now in Asia Minor, now in Macedonia, and then again in Athens, he viewed the Greek world with greater detachment and less bias than the pure Athenians, Plato and Isocrates. Having developed from the hard training school of later Platonic dialectic into an analyst of all forms of life and activity in their living development towards an end which they were destined to reach, he classified the five hundred years of Greek life from Homer to his own day with a penetration which makes his diagnosis applicable to other times and other civilisations, although in considering the validity of his prescribed cures we must always make due allowance for changes in social and historical conditions.

XI

CONCLUSION

THIS book is designed to be a modest contribution to present-day problems. Our way of life can only survive in the modern world if we are prepared to assert openly our ideals and our principles—the principles which are common ground for all political parties and the ideals for which we fought in both wars. The new factor, which has become clear in the last twenty years with the rise of Nazi Germany, Fascist Italy, and Communist Russia, is the assault of the totalitarians on the inner citadel of democracy, the totalitarian claim to be the true democracy because equality of opportunity is assured in the totalitarian state. The issue has therefore changed ; our belief in equality of opportunity is as strong as ever and our social legislation must be directed towards its realisation, but what distinguishes our way of life from the totalitarian way of life is not this belief, but the belief in the value of the individual—the right of the individual to freedom of speech and action, the right of the amateur to criticise the expert, and the right of the ordinary citizen to criticise and, if need be, overthrow the government. This is our essential belief : every man has a right to complete freedom of speech and as much freedom of action as is consonant with his fellows having an equal quantity, every man has a right to make his voice heard in public affairs, and the judgment of the expert, at least in broad matters of policy, must be submitted to the amateur for approval because the amateur knows better than the expert whether the plans which the expert formulates will work for ordinary people.

The moment of greatest interest to us in Greek history is the moment of full democracy, not only because of the political achievement, but because it was accompanied by a crisis in ethical thought following on a period of great scientific development which presents an obvious analogy to the present day. In spite of the difference in scale and complication, the fundamental problems of Periclean Athens were very like ours. Modern technical developments have in many ways compensated for the difference in scale. The introduction of machinery has made, or should soon make, it possible for every man to have the leisure which Aristotle desiderates for a citizen. Improved communications—railways, telephone, broadcasting, books, newspapers—make it possible for a Cabinet Minister to be as well known to 50,000,000 people to-day as he could be to 10,000 in Aristotle's time. While therefore the difference of scale and complication must never be forgotten, as far as the essential problems are concerned they do not constitute a difference in kind.

If we believe that the basis of sound government is the approval of the ordinary citizen and that this approval is the essential safeguard of the freedom of the individual, what is the answer to those who say that the rejection of traditional religion and the corruption of moral standards as a result of the growth of science has vitiated that approval by making it entirely an expression of self-interest, answered inevitably by the exacerbation of the possessing classes, who will defend their position even at the expense of acting as a fifth column for a foreign power? These are the terms in which Thucydides, the Old Oligarch, Plato, and Aristotle saw Athenian politics of the last quarter of the fifth century B.C. The dangers of an uneducated electorate voting for its immediate material advantage are clear; the results were the political disaster of defeat in war followed by a fascist revolution and by a counter-revolution with the suppression of certain outstanding individuals such as Socrates.

But in spite of the general truth of this diagnosis (and the disease can be seen persisting through the fourth century), certain ideas in democratic Athens suggest remedies which are of universal application. One of these is the idea of *nomos*, which survived the justifiable attacks of scientists and sophists on its foundations, *nomos* as the living tradition of Athenian law, institutions, customs, and beliefs, which guides the amateur judgment and is gradually remodelled to new conditions by the wise statesman, a tradition of tolerance and fairness and free discussion. This idea was the fundamental idea of the restored democracy of 403 B.C. and remained so through the fourth century, so that Demosthenes saw in *nomos*, imposed with the people's consent and supported by the people's will, the cause of the city's blessings. One element in this living Athenian tradition or *nomos* is *homonoia* or *philanthropia*, the unanimity which holds the classes of the Athenian state together and the humanity which makes Athens the champion of the oppressed and which finds practical expression in the humane treatment of slaves and foreigners in Athens, a humanity which Athens gave to the Hellenistic world and which made the Hellenistic world a possible cradle for Christianity. These conceptions survive and develop, although their original divine sanction was annihilated by the sophists; other permanent sanctions are found in the constitution of the human soul, in the age and venerability or in the universal and international character of the root ideas from which these conceptions are elaborated.

The idea of political excellence (*arete*), the disinterested ability and idealism of Solon, Pericles, and Demosthenes, which alone deserves honour and privilege and must be given honour and privilege, and the idea of *paideia* (education by environment, nurse and tutor, school and university, and the traditions of the state) both for the ordinary citizen, who votes at elections and sits on juries, and for the administrator and politician, have a similar fundamental importance. The Greeks saw clearly that, whether we like it or not, the citizen will be educated by all the sights and sounds that surround him from birth upwards and therefore the question is not Education or No Education, but Good Education or Bad Education. Pericles meant Athens to be an education for Greece, and Protagoras saw that the final and universal educator was the Athenian tradition or *nomoi*, but Plato must be given full credit for conceiving a system of state education both for the ordinary citizen and for the few suitably gifted to become administrators. He saw clearly that the whole quality of the state depended on its education. The tradition of the country is the most universal educator, but it must be (and here, I think, Protagoras and Aristotle would be nearer to us than Plato) a living tradition which is moulded to changing conditions by the wisdom of the statesman and approved by the amateur judgment of the ordinary citizen. *Paideia* has the double task of training both the statesman and the ordinary citizen, both deeply rooted in tradition, but both bold to adapt tradition to contemporary needs. One of the central ideas of the tradition itself must be the readiness to recognise *arete* wherever it arises, to give it the utmost freedom to develop, and to reward its success; this is the true meaning of equality of opportunity.

This view of life was first discovered, realised, and recorded by the ancient Greeks. At three moments in the history of the Western world the Greek contribution has been essential—first, the discovery itself· and the recording of it in worthy and ever-living literary forms ; secondly, the provision of forms of language and thought in which the early Christian thinkers could express themselves and the atmosphere in which to promulgate the gospel, and thirdly, the provision of examples and inspiration for the rebirth and regrowth of democracy from the time of the Tudors till the present day : it is pleasant and perhaps not wholly fanciful to regard the classical architecture of many of our public buildings as a symbolical acknowledgment of this debt.

I believe that a fourth such moment has arrived to-day and that a renewed study of ancient Greece is necessary if we are to reformulate our ideals to meet the conditions of the modern world. There we can see the battles that were fought by those who discovered individual freedom, and just because two thousand years and more separate us from the Greeks the un-essentials have faded out of the picture and the remaining lines have the clear and essential beauty of a geometrical diagram.

INDEX

Chief passages in *italics*

147

Printed in Great Britain by Butler & Tanner Ltd., Frome and London